Praise for I Give you My Word

This book is an ode to friendship! *I Give You My Word* is a celebration of the musings, the questions, and the knowings we offer each other through words. And it is a reminder of how the words of a friend can accompany, unveil and ignite both who we truly are and who we are wanting to become.

— **Jennifer Brooks Quinn**, Biographical Counselor and Adult Educator

These very human voices gave rise to memories of my own along with thoughts of those things that have changed and those that have not - yet. Most of all I am left with the certainty of our need for one another and how the strength of one circle of friends, sharing the essential questions of life, has the power to reach out across the world to create more connections and to touch the lives of so many.

— **Patricia Rubano**, Director, Biography and Social Art Program

Imagine finding a box of old letters — reading the exchanges between friends from almost 50 years ago and hearing your own voice back then. This book reminds readers of the joy of receiving letters, the benefits of life-long friendships, and the historic changes women were faced with in the 1970s. Lovely journey to "back in the day."

— **Patti Smith**, Facilitator, Center for Courage and Renewal and Center for Biography and Social Art

Also by Signe Eklund Schaefer

Why on Earth?
Biography and the Practice of Human Becoming

More Lifeways —
Finding support and inspiration in family life
(Co-edited with Patti Smith)

Ariadne's Awakening —
Taking up the Threads of Consciousness
(with Margli Matthews and Betty Staley)

I Give You My Word

Women's Letters as Life Support, 1973–1987

Page and cover design by Anna Myers Sabatini

Library of Congress Control Number: 2019937455
ISBN: 978-1-7328414-3-7

Schaefer, Signe.
I give you my word : women's letters as life support, 1973-1987 /
Signe Eklund Schaefer.
Housatonic, Massachusetts : Green Fire Press, [2019], ©2019.
340 pages : 1 illustration ; 13.335 cm x 20.32 cm
9781732841437
1. Schaefer, Signe — Correspondence. 2. Sex role. 3. Women —
Socialization. 4. Feminism. 5. Women — Social life and customs.
HQ1075 .S43 2019

305.3 (23 ed.)

Green
Fire
Press

I Give You My Word

Women's Letters as Life Support, 1973–1987

Signe Eklund Schaefer

Green Fire Press
Housatonic, Massachusetts

Dedication

To my friends of long ago and today

and also

To Friendship Itself

I Give You My Word

Women's Letters as Life Support, 1973–1987

Hundreds of letters
in a long forgotten box
testaments of youth
and striving to become

Old women now
and some of us gone
beyond a letter's reach

What shall I do
with this treasure
these crinkling blue leaves
telling in faded ink
our dreams and sufferings
our loves and longings
this rare and precious post
from days beyond remembering

2016

Table of Contents

If I want to understand what moves me, what confuses me, what pains me — everything that makes me react, in short — I have to put it into words. . . . Writing is my only way of absorbing and organizing life.

— Jhumpa Lahiri

The world is so empty if one thinks of only mountains and rivers and cities; but to know someone who thinks and feels with us and who, though distant is close to us in spirit, this makes the earth for us an inhabited garden.

— J. W. von Goethe

Introduction

"I have spent hours on this letter and I must stop. I can't believe I have written as much as I have — of course there is so much more I would like to say...."

A few years ago, as I was rummaging in my attic, I saw a large box that had been pushed into a dark corner behind baskets of toys now forgotten by even my grandchildren, plastic bins of unsorted photographs, and boxes of books which should have been given away long ago but for lingering family nostalgia. I had no idea what was in that closed-up, unmarked box, and I remember approaching it as if it might hold some long-buried treasure. And truly it did! As I carefully opened the top, I saw that the box was full of letters — letters from my women friends in the 1970's, when I lived in England. Shuffling quickly through the piles of blue airmail envelopes, I saw that there were also many from the 1980's, after my family had returned to the United States.

How could these letters have been unknowingly saved for all these decades? Years in which our family had changed homes at least ten times, living in three different countries as well as three states. My husband and I have moved too many times in our long life together to be hoarders, so how did this box survive unnoticed? And not only how, but why? At the very least, it seemed that this surprising discovery offered me an opportunity to look back on an extremely important time in my life, from age 28 until 42. Very soon, it became clear to me that this was about something larger than only my own reminiscences.

I should say that even in my childhood, my family moved a lot. Before high school, I had lived in the east, west, middle and south of the US, as well as in South America. Letters had been very important for me since I was a little girl. My father travelled a great deal, and letters from and to him helped me to feel our connection. With our many family moves, I also wanted to keep in touch with friends. Although many younger people today may not have any direct experience of writing or receiving letters, for me letter writing was a well-established habit by the time I went off to college.

In 1973, my husband and I, with our two young children, moved to England for further study. Our initial plan was to be gone for one year, but we ended up staying for eight years, with some of that time also spent in the Netherlands. First I was a student, but later both my husband and I were on the faculty of Emerson College, an international center in Forest Row, Sussex, based on the work of Rudolf Steiner.[1] Steiner referred to his work as spiritual science, or Anthroposophy (from the Greek *anthropos* meaning human being, and *Sophia,* the name for divine wisdom). Adult students, most of whom had already completed university, came to Emerson from all over the world to study Steiner's ideas and their practical manifestations in Waldorf Education, Bio-dynamic Agriculture, Social Development, and several different artistic practices.

I formed deep and lasting friendships during this time in England. Some of those friends returned to their own countries after they, or their husbands, finished their studies. And so the flow of letters intensified beyond the old friends in the US with whom I was still in touch. Eventually, in 1981, our family moved back to the States — first to Detroit, Michigan and four years later to Spring

---

1   Rudolf Steiner (1861–1925) was an Austrian philosopher, social reformer and spiritual researcher whose work has had a lasting influence on cultural renewal since the beginning of the 20th century, for example through Waldorf Education, Biodynamic agriculture, and Anthroposophical medicine. He was also active in a broad spectrum of artistic disciplines. He wrote and lectured extensively, and articulated a path of spiritual development premised on and supportive of individual freedom and responsibility. As a western esoteric teacher he described his modern spiritual science, or Anthroposophy, as "a path of knowledge to guide the spiritual in the human being to the spiritual in the universe."

Valley, New York. The letters in my treasure box span 1973 to 1987 — new writers came along throughout those years, while a few fell away with time. And some were consistently there.

The 1970's were particularly exciting years for young women in many parts of the world, but certainly in America and England. We felt ourselves capable of things our mothers could only dream about — we wanted to find meaningful work in fields that were only slowly creaking open to women. Many of us had read *The Feminine Mystique* in college — I received it as a high school graduation gift from my mother! In the '70's most of my friends and I were mothers of young children, and we took our mothering very seriously. But we also wanted to study or find challenging part-time work, something that was often quite difficult, given the options for child care then, perhaps especially in small-town England.

At that time I had a deepening interest in both the emerging women's movement and the ideas of Rudolf Steiner's spiritual science. I felt sure that these two fields had something important to say to each other. After many hours of enlivening conversation, my friend Christa Kaufmann and I put up a notice at the local college, inviting other women to join us in forming a group where we could consider, from our own experiences, the questions being raised by women at that time. We had the added goal of exploring those questions from a perspective that included ideas about the evolution of human consciousness and the importance of pursuing an individual path of inner development. Our search would be founded on the conviction that an invisible world of spiritual activity was as real as the visible, material world available to our senses.

Within a couple of months, there were two groups meeting weekly, and as the years went by, these groups multiplied. Many participants were students at the college and so would take part for a year or two before going back to their own countries. As they returned home, several initiated similar groups with whom we kept in contact — in Holland, Germany, the US, Australia, and other parts of England. Some members of the two original groups lived in the local village on a more long-term basis. After the first year, we joined together, continuing to meet for several more years. In 1977 this group decided to give the growing work a name.

We chose the name Ariadne — after the maiden in Greek mythology who offered a golden thread of awakening consciousness to her wandering hero lover, Theseus. At that point, we were mostly busy being mothers at home, but we were also passionate about what we were discovering. We gradually began to realize we were training ourselves for some future work in the world. As the years went by, we started holding workshops and offering classes. We published a newsletter and did an incredible amount of research — into history, mythology, feminism, psychology, spirituality, and ourselves. In time, much of our research was published in *Ariadne's Awakening: Taking up the Threads of Consciousness,* with chapters by Margli Matthews, Betty Staley and myself (Hawthorn Press, 1986). As different members of the original groups moved around the world, many of our letters addressed this developing work. In Chapter 5, "Finding ourselves — Finding Our Work," there is more about Ariadne, both the story and the growing work.

All through those years, I was receiving letters — from old friends back in the States and from friends who had moved on from their time in England. Eventually, I, too, moved on, and then the letters came also from England. The letters speak of our longings and our discoveries, of our love for our children and our commitments to our marriages. They are full of questions, worries, disappointments, and hopes. They are a record of an important transition time in history — many things were changing for women, for men, for families, and in the working world as well.

The letters also give images of a particular time in a woman's life. Most of us were between our late twenties and our early forties during the years these letters were written. In anyone's life, these are significant years of finding oneself as an adult, perhaps as a partner, a parent, a colleague, and a member of a broader community. They are years of discovery, experimentation, pursuing dreams and experiencing setbacks. Although many of us were wanderers, these are also years of settling down, if not in an outer location and home, then at least within one's sense of self as a maturing adult.[2]

Recalling those years of receiving, and writing, so many letters led me to ask myself: what is a letter actually? In a personal — as opposed to business — sense, at its simplest, a letter is an exchange of news, ideas, questions and support between friends. The letters in my box were handwritten, mostly on both sides of thin, translucent airmail paper. They were hard to read even when they first arrived, and, of course, harder now with older eyes and faded ink. But even after all these years, the still recognizable handwriting on the different pages conjures up the unique individualities of my friends. We were quite literally impressing our very selves onto the pages. These letters were written before the days of computers, breezy emails, or word-contracting texts. In recent decades, we have come to rely ever more on email and texting, and our exchanges tend to be quickly done, brief and succinct. These expansive letters were filled with heart.

Writing a real letter took time. As a young mother who eventually also had an ever more demanding career,

---

2   For a more detailed description of different life phases, see my book *Why on Earth? — Biography and the Practice of Human Becoming*, Steiner Books, 2013. Life Phases are also discussed in *Phases* by Bernard Lievegoed, *Taking Charge* by Gudrun Burkhard, and many other sources referenced in *Why on Earth?*

I remember the terrible frustration of not finding free moments in my busy days in which to sit with paper and pen and enter into a conversation with a distant friend. Days and weeks could go by until finally a free hour presented itself or I simply forced myself to make time to write, even if it meant sacrificing sleep. Many letters, both to me and from me, were written in installments stretching over several days, and many went on for 20 or 30 pages. In my box, I found two that actually topped 40 pages!

There were stops and starts and important realizations along the way. That's the thing about writing letters: the very act served as a pause in the on-rush of life — a moment for self-reflection that often led to some new discovery. Writing a letter invited a sifting of priorities, and the sharing of parts of oneself that might never take the stage in everyday life. With each friendship there might be only two or three of these long letters in a whole year, but they confirmed a trusted connection that reached across time and space. Sitting with one's friend in mind and heart was an act of attention and care — both for the friend and for oneself. A letter would bring the friend into heart focus and could also open questions for both the writer and the recipient. For a moment, a doorway could unlock into the self that was too often kept shut by the requirements of busy days.

Receiving a letter was its own special joy. Time had to stop for its reading. Stolen moments — shushing the children, turning off the stove, maybe even hiding in the bathroom to open those fat envelopes. Unfolding the crinkly thin pages felt like taking hold of a lifeline, something I experienced as vital to my becoming. International telephone calls — of course always on land line phones, often with long coiling wires — were expensive in the 1970's and so letters, however infrequent, were an intimate way of addressing a yearning to be connected as conscious, contributing and free-spirited women.

Many letters began with an apology: "*I've been trying to write you all summer…*" or "*Sorry I'm using a pencil but the dog ate my only pen and if I go in the other room I'll wake the baby.*" They meandered through bone-deep exhaustion and heart-aching love for children, worries about health or aging parents, or the struggle to find real work. There were hopes, and odd dreams, sorrows and small joys. There were questions about, and warm greetings for each other's families. And again and again the underlined question: *What am I meant to be learning?* Of course, relationships filled many pages — the challenges with husbands, the self-doubts as wives, but also the fierce hopes for meaning in the struggle to forge a conscious relationship of equals.

Apologies also showed up in familiar endings, "*I must stop, or I'll fall asleep. This is, of course, nothing like what I intended to write, but I'll mail it, because it's something.*" There is great humor in the letters and ongoing revelations of parts of oneself that might never have showed up in the everyday exchanges of friends who live close to each other. One envelope has a long note covering most of the back with things needing to be added after the letter was sealed, and then along the side edge was written, *"Did you know I was the type that wrote on the outside of envelopes?"*

When women friends talk with each other, the conversations are often multi-dimensional. There may be an abundance of factual details — the color of a newly painted wall, the look on a child's face as she ties her first shoe, the experience of being invisible at a meeting with mostly men — but interlaced with the facts are also expressions of how things felt, questions getting clearer, and even barely articulated hopes. Women are willing to jump levels with each other without needing to go immediately to "but what's the point?" They can laugh and cry without feeling a contradiction. And there is an abundance of support for the other. Within the conversation, the relationship itself is being honored and nurtured.

I mention women's conversations — admittedly making broad-stroke generalizations — because of something that particularly moved me about the letters I found. In our everyday lives we have no record of the depth and breadth of how women friends speak with each other, but these letters clearly capture something on paper that is otherwise so ephemeral. Here are women — thousands of miles away from each other — trying to 'talk,' to nurture a living conversation, sharing from their hearts, holding the other with love and respect, working to actively support who the friend is becoming.

As I was reading through the letters, I began to hear what I came to think of as a kind of collective voice of that time as I remember it playing out in my own life. Almost any one of my friends, or even I myself, could have written what actually came from someone else — not in terms of the details of course, but as an articulation of the sorts of events, questions and challenges that, each in our own way, all of us were experiencing. I wondered if this voice might not also speak for, and to, others; and so I began to type excerpts from the different letters into broadly themed files such as relationships, motherhood, children, letter writing, finding oneself, finding work, inner development, general musings, and several others. All of this stretched out over many months, and I was not really concerned whether I was doing this just for myself or for some broader purpose. Simultaneously I began to read my own sporadic journals from those years and I realized that many of the entries were what I would surely have written about in my letters to friends. Although I did not have my own letters, I did have this record of my impressions, thoughts, concerns, and questions from those years. So I began to put some of these journal entries into my files, as well.

One day when I was driving, not thinking about the letters at all, suddenly the title — *I Give You My Word* — dropped into my consciousness. With what I can only describe as a quickening heart, I felt the possibility of this book jump into focus. That is what my friends and I were doing: offering each other our words, with all the authenticity and truth that we had within us. Letters were what allowed us to discover and fulfill the promise of our connection, to continue to serve our friendship even when we could have no way of knowing how, or even if, we would ever be able to see each other in the future. In the years of these letters we had scattered far: throughout England, Australia, Europe, and across the States from New York to California. I am very grateful to say that most of the friends whose words I have included in this book are still in my life. We now use phones, email, and happily, occasional visits to continue nurturing our still long-distance relationships.

As I mentioned, for most people letters stopped being a main source of long-distance communication a few decades ago. When I think how important writing and receiving letters has been for me, I wonder what other people who are living far away from friends do now. Obviously there is email and the phone, and of course texting, Instagram and tweets, as well as Skype, Facetime, or other 'chatting' technologies; but where is the opportunity to quietly reflect on what one wants to share with one particular person, or what the other might need to hear? Is re-reading a text as nourishing as re-reading a 25-page letter? Of course we adapt to what is available, and we can try to bring care into any kind of communication, but this needs real consciousness.

It recently occurred to me that the rise in journaling classes and memoir workshops might be a contemporary replacement for what letter writing used to offer to the writer. These are certainly important invitations to reflect on one's life, thoughts and feelings, and the events that have been formative in how we come to understand ourselves.

But the focus in journal and memoir writing tends to be primarily on oneself, whereas a letter is invariably also concerned with the relationship between the letter writer and the recipient. With a letter we reach out of ourselves, we direct our attention toward a real and known other.

I am sorry that letter writing has gone out of vogue, because the importance of the other is so clear. Even when letter writers are expressing things about themselves, it is within the context of the relationship. The writer could try out an idea secure in the knowledge that the other would receive it as a gift, to be opened, turned over and examined, and then, in time, a reply might come back. In writing to a friend, you would try to see the other in your mind's eye, and you would know that they also saw you. I mean this in the fullest sense of the word "see": the building of a clear inner image and also the activity of open-heartedly accepting and valuing the other — and feeling known, accepted, valued and held with all the messiness of your emerging self and also the potential only just beginning to bud.

In the following chapters, there are no names or identifying characteristics that would allow readers to follow the particular personalities and stories of my friends. I decided that to attach names — even fictional ones — to the many excerpts would be a distraction from the collective voice that I came to experience as I read the letters. I realize that, initially, this may be frustrating for readers because it is natural to want to know how a specific event, question or reflection plays out over time. It asks readers to read differently, not looking for individual stories with clear plot lines unfolding through the years. I hope that a collective voice will sound through the many words, and will awaken an enhanced sense of that particular time in history and of important experiences in everywoman's life.

Of course each of my friends has a fascinating, unique biography and their life circumstances during those years were obviously different. Picture, for example, a recent transplant to England, married with two small children but still feeling the energy of her college years in the States during the turbulent 1960's. Or a former math student working in the exciting new computer industry, on the surface so unlike the daughter of the British upper class who relinquished that life to pursue Waldorf education. Or a California girl in Laura Ashley dresses and a growing brood of children clinging to her long skirts. There was an aspiring young farmer with a new husband and an expressive, inventive use of words that could make a sailor blush. Very different was the gentle Chinese chemist devoted to her laboratory research, or the depressed single mother unable to find a job with enough scope for her unquenchable creativity.

The writers of these letters were married, single, mothers, teachers, farmers, women in business, living in various countries. Taken together their words express directly, warmly and with integrity the complexity of those times and the need we felt for each other. As already mentioned, I have also included excerpts from my own journals in those years. In addition, I found I had a few letters that I wrote to my sister — these were given back to me after she died several years ago. I have included a few passages from them, as well as others from a couple of letters returned to me by one friend. All together there are words from twenty-one writers. From some there are only a few paragraphs, and from others many more; but each voice plays an important part in the sounding of the whole composition.

In each chapter, the excerpts are arranged in chronological groupings, beginning in 1973 and ending in 1987. Deciding which paragraphs to put into which chapter was sometimes immediately obvious and other times quite a challenge. It will be clear that some could have been placed in more than one chapter. The letters themselves often meandered along a lively stream of consciousness, dipping through overlapping thoughts and feelings, jumping from the bane of laundry to a deep philosophical perplexity. Sometimes I have interrupted the writer's flow and separated out themes. Other times the spontaneous complexity remains with all its multi-dimensional brilliance. I can imagine that occasionally the movement through the different excerpts may feel jumpy — perhaps not unlike the roaming, distractible nature of our own individual inner lives.

The first chapter consists of general musings on a wide variety of subjects and as such lacks a thematic flow. Among the variety of offerings, topics are sounded that will be deepened in later chapters. The next four chapters address primary interests and concerns in our daily lives: motherhood and children, relationships, inner and outer development, and finding ourselves and our work. Chapter 6 looks at letter writing itself and how through letters we became more conscious of the importance of our friendships.

Many of the letters are full of dots, dashes, underlinings, capital letters and parentheses. I have converted the latter to dashes because in my effort to shield the writers from being identified, I have used parentheses to remove names and condense unnecessary details. Aside from this and an occasional 'a' or 'the' or a shift in tense for clarity, I have made no other changes in my friends' words. My own commentary along the way is in bold print.

The words that follow are the long ago offerings of my very articulate and much loved friends.

CHAPTER I

Musings on Matters Large and Small

This first chapter of excerpts gives a broad picture of the kinds of things my friends and I had on our minds in those years during the '70's and '80's of the last century. Many of the concerns expressed are quite particular to our daily lives — to shave or not to shave our legs, the role of gossip, the difficulties of moving to a new community or even a new country. Others show their universal nature more directly — care for economic issues, experiences of prejudice, efforts toward peace. The very first excerpt anticipates the need for the #MeToo movement by almost fifty years. There are questions of how to celebrate festivals as our children grow older, and ponderings on the changing nature of 'fun' as we were growing older. Some writers shared what they were reading, or what they had encountered when traveling.

Many of these excerpts could have fit easily into later chapters — and indeed, several of the themes touched here will be deepened in other parts of the book. Yet placed together here, I hope these passages show the multi-dimensional state of body, soul, and spirit of a certain collection of women who were trying to bring consciousness to our lives in the middle of the second half of the twentieth century. Included here are individual reflections on our experiences as women at a pivotal time for women. The writings reach far and wide, and also touch closely what is near and dear.

1973 – 1975

I think you should definitely give (your boss) a good silent stab with the elbow the next time he comes up behind you! And just ask him to be quiet when he has nothing but garbage to say.

*

By the way, I still shave my legs — I tried not, but found it uncomfortable and unattractive. I may be socially brainwashed but I still don't really like hairiness! Many of my friends don't shave though.

I Give You My Word

*

After a visit by the wife of an older colleague of her husband's:

A kind woman and I enjoyed talking to her. She doesn't seem to be upset by it, but I feel her life would be/have been so sad for me — husband always away, leaving places she loved. She talks of the importance of being home for your children and I agree yet feel there must be more. Yet she seems genuine and honest and not bitter in her feelings of service to husband and home.

Can I find some right kind of balance for me? Some objective understanding of why I am a woman and what I have to do during this life? What I can do, should do, must do?

*

I haven't felt pressured this week in my evening pursuits — is this my old laziness reasserting itself or is it right that I quietly move around among only three basic activities — reading Parsifal, studying (a foreign language), and writing letters? I think it is better that I didn't begin three books and several assorted projects but still I have to always be careful that I don't just do things that I instinctively enjoy.

*

My mother will like this house we live in now but it just doesn't fit me — I'm not really comfortable in such a 'nice' neighborhood.

*

I have decided that, women's lib aside, women are indeed intuitive — and much more so than men. It astounds me how long, for example, (two men friends) can spend logically coming up with some 'truth' which is simply obvious to me from the start. I know I must learn to go into my intuitions and find reasons for things I feel are right, but surely this does not mean endless time spent on belaboring the obvious?

*

This writer could not have imagined the changes that the coming decades would bring to the land she was visiting — in fact, a country that no longer exists as it was structured and called in 1974.

We had a good vacation, it was very nice to get away and certainly interesting in Czechoslovakia, but so depressing. The country is so run down, so neglected — dirty, broken, half-finished. The people look totally lethargic as they move along the streets — you feel the weight of an external crush on the spirit of a whole people. I didn't expect to see abundant prosperity, but I didn't expect such a feeling of defeat either. All the lovely old buildings of Prague — the splendor that must have been — are black with neglect and/or misuse. Beautiful old churches are often now used as state museums — of course extolling the virtues of the Communist State.

On the way to Prague, we picked up three hitchhikers — three Czechs, recent graduates in economics from the University in Prague. As it turned out, we couldn't get a hotel room and we ended up spending two days with one of the young men we picked up. This gave us a much realer insight into the situation and problems. Jan's father is a retired Army Major, was a party member from 1948 to 1968 when he was kicked out — not loyal enough to the Russian invasion. He was very warm and friendly to us — but still not able to discuss the — obvious — fact that there are very real problems in the country. Jan, on the other hand, hates the Russians, says he will never join the party although he knows it will mean he can never have a really good or for him meaningful job. He was so earnest, and so sad — and it's so hard to imagine what kind of a future he has. Yet he won't leave because he feels Czechoslovakia is his country. I really got very depressed by the whole sadness of it all.

*

All the heaviness of all the possible choices in life weigh on me very heavily and I find it hard to physically move — to decide — I'd like to have a better sense of freedom and spontaneity — a better sense of life and light and hope for a better world. I see pollution and have trouble breathing — I see inflation and have trouble buying the necessities to live — I see and feel and hear dissension, depression and despair in others around me — I worry about a 3rd World War and complete pain and annihilation. My senses are battered constantly by unsolicited noises from traffic, radios and television and newspapers — and they all really scare me and help to keep me bound and tight with apprehension. I don't live well in this world.

*

I've been thinking about gossip and the aspects and necessity of it. It serves as a will exercise to control the amount and intensity of it. It does a lot of bad things when it's out of control and deliberate, but it also does this: people want to touch the problem areas that they have and to have them acknowledged as problems, but sometimes not as their own. I think my mother does a lot of this in her debates and discussions. The problems are universal and so can be expounded upon in a general, gossip fashion.

*

Our bedroom ceiling is fixed. And it looked so nice we got inspired to paint the whole room and it really looks good. There is one lilac wall and also the doors (4) of a big ugly built-in closet on the opposite wall. It's a great soft color. We picked it because I found some remnant fabric in my favorite colors (blues and purples) and so decided to make new curtains. The gold brocade uglies that were there were too bad for words. The windows are around a big seat-like extension out of the room, looking out on the garden. I think I will eventually turn it into a seat with some pillows. Anyway, I'm glad now the ceiling fell in because it all looks so much nicer.

✳

By the way, "heavy" is one of my favorite words! Especially as applied to some (people) and even to our own lives sometimes. We seem to always be so serious. It isn't good to <u>always</u> be heavy! Happily I retain my irreverent streak and have decided to — I'm willing to suffer for it next time!! Actually though, we sometimes realize that it's not easy to have 'fun' anymore — that is, the old ways don't always seem as pleasurable and we haven't yet come up with completely new ways. But I do believe the new ways must exist.

✳

An interesting theme that pops up occasionally in the letters — also in excerpts in later chapters — is the idea of reincarnation. For some of my friends, and for me as well, the possibility of repeated earth lives

23

was something we took very seriously. The letters raise questions about whether there is some kind of pre-birth intentionality underlying our relationships and experiences — the suggestion that we encounter certain people and situations as a deliberate invitation to further development. We were exploring the idea that the outcome of such meetings was not fixed or pre-determined, but that the opportunity in the encounter might hold intention and meaning from what one could call our higher — or more eternal — self.

While I was looking into *Theosophy* (by Rudolf Steiner), I came upon something that really clicked with all that I had been thinking. It was a section on selflessness and the need to develop it — of course an idea I have 'heard' a million times. But this time I thought — oh, my God — that is why I had to be a woman this time — in my experience as a woman I am forced by 'reality' to be more selfless — i.e. more than I like — not to mention martyrdom. My reality is thoroughly intertwined with my husband and the children in a way that is much stronger than, for instance, my husband's to me and the children. Perhaps I was very strong-willed and selfish last time and as a man this time, I might not have been inclined to strive after 'selflessness,' but as a woman I have the opportunity to experience it (at least conceptually) in a very real way, and perhaps learn to develop it.

Here come the kids — more later.

✻

Can girls be brought up with truly equal intellectual opportunity and yet not experience conflict/resentment/loss of self at being a wife and mother? How can higher education foster individual development rather than skill competition?

✻

The funny — not ha! ha! — thing is that being here isn't at all what we 'want' — it came about because of what (my husband) felt was a real need. When this need stops needing, we will move on to another one some place else. It's sometimes hard — perhaps especially for me — to be so removed from my previous ideas of time and space and the realities of people I love — but that's the way it is. So I try to understand what this sense of 'homelessness' means — what I can learn from it — some days with greater success than others!

✻

The trip back yesterday was grueling — we got off 45 minutes late because the car wouldn't start and so I had to drive hard to make the boat on time. Then there were about 500 — exaggeration! — English school children — age 12 to 14 — on the boat and the last two hours were very rough and I swear two-thirds of them were sick! My son loved it, my daughter was a bit melodramatic, but finally fell asleep and I kept telling myself "mind above matter!" We finally got to Dover and off the boat into a dilly of a snowstorm and the usual awful English roads. It was altogether charming, but I made it home with a certain sense of accomplishment!

✳

In 1975, this friend was working at a large international bank, in a challenging and exciting management position. She felt she had the opportunity to make an impact on traditional attitudes since she had a level of responsibility that offered much room for innovation and accomplishment. There was such idealism in what she shared. And in several excerpts that follow this one, other friends reflect on being a woman or on the need for and nature of 'the feminine.' There will be more on this subject in Chapter 5.

I really identified with your comments regarding women and 'liberation.' Since coming to California, I have devoted much energy to developing a closeness and communication with other women. It seems that it is a very recent phenomenon that women have started to open up and be willing to discuss potentially painful topics. So many of the women I had met since college lacked such confidence in themselves that they avoided exploring alternatives. They had resigned themselves to their 'lot' in life. There was little trust among women too — a carry over from competitive struggles over men.

One thing that is so common among women is that each of us thinks that because we have questionings and doubts and failures with traditionally accepted roles that there is something uniquely wrong with us. For so long, women perpetuated these very roles for fear of being exposed as a failure or as weird — problems with sex, problems with coping — with husbands, with feelings of meaninglessness, with children, etc. It is such a revelation to each of us as we realize finally that all of us share similar feelings of inadequacy. Once this hurdle is overcome — trust, real communication — it is possible for women to open, to re-establish their self-confidence and to take positive steps toward unlimited growth and expansion of self. And this is a <u>very exciting</u> happening.

I agree with you totally regarding the 'Women's Lib' movement. It carries such overtones of negativism toward men as our oppressors. We, ourselves, are also our oppressors. It is time for 'liberation' of both men and women. And I see it taking place all around me. It is an exciting time to be alive.

Women *now* carry responsibility to develop and consciously recognize these (needed) feminine traits because we carry the 'image'—the form most connected to them. We must not neglect our other sides either, but we must nurture and, carry into the world, these special feminine traits lest they be forgotten. If we as women believe in what we feel we have/are developing, then we must take some first steps. It is our responsibility because these new capabilities are open to us.

*

If you ever jot down some of your thoughts, I'd love to read them. I'm tired of reading about neurotic people who have allowed themselves to become victims of society — even if the story is well-worth repeating — because I don't think all people are like that and just once, I'd like a stronger character to make an appearance. If I were a novelist, I'd write such a story. But, fortunately I don't delude myself about having abilities that just aren't there. But I keep wondering if there is some way of evening the balance. Maybe you can do it?

*

In our group, we discussed the question of whether women are unconsciously prejudiced by feeling that women are not 'creative' — i.e. in a man's world — politics, science, art, etc... I certainly feel something worked in me — but is 'prejudice' only one, rather simple, way of expressing this? Could it be something basically healthy which protects the 'feminine' within one from being swamped by an animus-type creativity — protects not only for feminine roles — motherhood, etc — but also for the *possibility* of some more real creativity — out of feminine and masculine sides in a conscious balance: what Esther Harding calls "suprapersonal?"

＊

How can we reach a sense of "feminine essence?" Some say by building a connection to menstrual periods — meditation — going inward. In the past, tribeswomen left the tribe during their period. We 'go on' — but should we? What could be learned about spiritual connections at this time? Or, how can we work to articulate feelings — as important for ourselves and for men we relate to — face the difficulty of expressing, articulating really deep feelings — work through vulnerability, lack of clarity, need to be understood, the roles one plays… I have a feeling that men would rather let many things go — even if they see/feel them.

＊

Question of what is 'aggressive' in a woman — is it only because she is a woman that one applies this word? Would one say that of her if she were a man? Why are men, and women, intimidated by assertive women? Could — or should — the woman act otherwise?

＊

Where is the mystery between people — does it continually grow deeper as layers are removed? The problem of how to act when one strips away games, etiquette, and yet a new kind of meeting/relationship has not emerged. Or the problem of articulate, educated, intelligent, achieving women — is it our masculine side that wants recognition, honor, achievement in the eyes of the world?

✳

A woman friend asked, why must she with all her own silly idiosyncrasies represent some new impulse of women? The newness and importance could be so easily ignored by knocking her down for her own individual failings — and yet we must go on — and find our own balance so that we can bring something into the world.

✳

On a 30 day boat trip — from England to Australia

Every afternoon at 2:30 there is a discussion group. It first labored through all the well-known favorites — Euthanasia, Capitol Punishment, etc., but recently, more interestingly, 'The future of the family,' 'Women's Lib' — of course! 'Permissive society,' 'Destiny — Does it exist?' — !! — I went to the one on 'W.L' — I try to go to all, but usually the baby is awake, and my husband is asleep, so sometimes I don't manage... The 'W.L.' one was interesting at times. They threw discussion open to the floor at one stage. After one of the less intelligent men had said that, in his opinion, women were introverted, extroverted, illogical, I decided it was time for something a bit more philosophical and introduced the idea of masculinity and femininity in all of us and the possibility of working to achieve balance. One oldish guy at the back called something out which I was meant not to hear, and I couldn't resist it — I stopped and said: "Do you wish to speak? Can I answer you in some way?" He mumbled and muttered and someone in the audience called out — "Come on, you gutless wonder," and the fun began. It was great, even if totally irrelevant. The obscenities, for the five minutes they lasted, were delicious. I maintained a dignified silence throughout and then resumed when the bumfight was over. The best and worst of Australia is so often manifest in these discussions. People get up and say, "I'm only a housewife and I've been married for 55 years, but..." Others are generous and insightful, with a particular brand of stoic understanding that I somehow recognize as Australian.

※

1976 – 1978

In the following excerpt there is reference made to 'elemental beings,' by which the writer means beings of nature who she feels enliven the earth, water, air and warmth — who infuse the natural world with living being.

Elemental beings are <u>so</u> present here. I always felt it. Before I used to say that <u>nature</u> was very omnipresent — probably something can't be <u>very</u> omnipresent — it either is, or it isn't, I guess. Now I feel it as Elementals — so close — often hard to handle. Often I feel as though I am walking in a Bosch landscape, complete. I'm <u>not</u> losing me marbles, either.

✳

To the question of in-depth thinking — women seem less inclined/able to do this. That is, we think flexibly, and with great insights — plunges to the depth — but do we lack the interest or ability to slow the steps of thinking down — prefer to jump in and out, touch much, but generally avoid conclusions and logic and what might seem 'plodding'? Do we actually fear to go the steps — will we lose our insight? Or might it be proven wrong? I see this play in many ways: in a group discussion where I 'know' the outcome early on and am bored while men plod on laboriously to the 'obvious' conclusion — they feel elated at the discovery of an outcome. I feel disgusted at the waste of time, *yet* I could *never* have articulated my early idea in a way that they could have then accepted. Why not? Or could I have if *rightly* done?

I find more difficult the conversations with men where women are required to explain, use more precise words, etc. than with other women. Yet we can learn more about 'clear thinking' in this kind of relationship.

Men can be very 'flexible,' aware, in their thinking when it is required of them. So, is this a particularly 'feminine' trait? Of teachers, group trainers? One man spoke of the difficulty of taking a lecture reading with a woman friend seriously.

✳

Often in the letters there would be exchanges about different possibilities for celebrating festivals, through the cycle of the year. We would write about things we were wondering about, or trying with our families, or questions that lived in us.

Advent: what is it really? Esoterically? What is the message for children? For family life? — how to bring it? Why has it been so lost in western culture? How can its meaning be re-awakened?

✳

I've been thinking about the preparation of Advent for children — needing to prepare to receive — "Love the guest is on the way"… The growing light of Advent candles — to a tree a-glow. Children experience through the physical, the spiritual reality. The concept of waiting — for Christmas, for anything — is so difficult for people now — carrying something within. I like the idea to build a story through the elements — earth, water, air, fire — and elementals on the four Sundays of Advent — i.e. about an old barn. Cleared out for something special, tied into bringing out the crèche — first empty, then bring hay, then animals, and finally people. As these things are done for the children, we can remember a now lost innocence — that is a part of us.

*

My husband was at a board meeting not so long ago, when the topic of the Spring Festival was raised. As has been done in the past, they once again imaginatively decided to read the Raphael Imagination (by Rudolf Steiner) and have supper afterwards. My husband came home and told me and I thought, "Right, that's IT!" By 10 a.m. the next morning, I'd virtually arranged the whole thing and was feeling really good — action suits me. A friend rang and I told her and she immediately offered lots of other good suggestions, so it just kept growing and now we're really excited because it really looks like a promising day. All I want is to be able to offer something that these people will <u>enjoy</u> and be enlivened by, that will somehow make their hearts LIVE and be lightened, even if it is only for a couple of hours.

*

The Spring Festival was very nice. I enjoyed undertaking that and it was humble enough, but a start… That book you sent me on the festivals really helped me to clarify lots of things I'd been dealing with, and it arrived at a most opportune time. I thanked you every time I read it, which was pretty often in the last few weeks. It's well written.

I Give You My Word

*

Discussing masculine/feminine balance with my husband, I said feminine must work out things — and take to the masculine — dependent *now* on the feminine. I said: "The ball rests in the feminine court." Not a bad pun!!

*

As you may know they have started construction on NH's first nuclear plant. It's right on the coast behind a resort town, most of whose inhabitants voted against having it there and of course were overruled. So for the last two years, people have periodically occupied and demonstrated... Several of us got training in non-violence and are going to camp out there for 4 days, with many others, next weekend. On one day there will be a mass rally; for the rest we want to have a presence there to focus attention on the issue. It's all strangely reminiscent of the 60's and the anti-war movement and yet there's also a completely different quality there. I've talked to several people about it and we all agree that the women's movement has really had a tremendous influence on the present approach. I would describe it as a rounding and humanizing influence, so that added to the tradition of non-violence already developed, there is much conscious effort made to care for and about one's neighbor, be he/she a fellow demonstrator or a policeman or the inhabitants, here, whose feelings are taken into consideration. There is much more respect for individual differences of lifestyle, dress, life philosophy, as opposed to informal regimentation. And much talk about one's 'center' being inviolable and really where it's at. Ironic that this year is the 10th anniversary of '68. Many of the people we met at the training had been active in the 60's. The women, particularly, described how much they had changed, so that now it was ok to be vulnerable, afraid, sensitive, caring, etc. Very interesting and also much more engaging for me. I feel I have a place there to be me.

✳

1979 – 1982

During these years, several people moved — sometimes to new countries — and eventually this was the case for my family as well. For me, this was a move back to the States after eight years in Europe. It definitely felt like the right step for our family, but it was still difficult to leave friends, the beginnings of work I loved, and a place that was dear to all of us. The various moves meant that a new group of writers began sending me letters. In addition, with our children now in elementary school, several of us had begun working at least part-time — some in self-created work. Many were active parents in their children's schools while others were busy founding new schools. Social and political issues of the times came ever more into the letters.

*

Well, we're here, have rented a house for the winter, have sort of settled in with some wonderfully varied household effects. Somebody — I can't remember who — is certain a dark green cane rocker used to belong to you. If so, I shall rock in it with even greater pleasure. The weather is beautiful, hot and cold bright days, leaves turning, high winds, and I can hardly believe how alien and at times merciless I feel the nature to be, as if, if you let up for a minute, it would or could crush you. I can hardly reconcile my superficial experience of it, glutting ourselves on corn, picking apples, walking in the sun and such beauty, with what I feel is just below the surface. It may be all my imagination and projection, because that's a bit how the whole experience of here is. So many fine people, the beginning of friendships, a certain ease in doing things, lovely food, scenery, architecture and yet, at times — or perhaps all the time underneath — a great loneliness and some fear. I miss you terribly. I miss us as a group, and at moments have such a hunger to be back with you. Those were such important times I had with you, and exchanges, and, of course, they live on in me as nourishment as much as pain that I can't have more now.

*

I don't know why we're here and can't possibly justify it — Why <u>don't</u> we go somewhere else? Apart from the obvious reason of not having money to get out, there would also be a feeling — for me, and I think, too, for my husband — of unfinishedness, of something — <u>what?</u> — undertaken and not completed. The time doesn't feel right to move on and yet I'm not committed to being here especially. Though it <u>looks</u> like I am. Do you know that feeling? Lots to be engaged in, lots of things to do, but doing them all because they need doing, not because it's what you especially want to do. One thing I am doing, that I <u>would</u> be really enthusiastic about <u>if</u> I really believed the right people were here to make it possible, is trying to establish a place where adults can come to experience an adult 'Waldorf education!' That's fumblingly put, but the best the group of people who are involved can do. I'm going to sound like a shit, but sometimes I go off my head at their slowness, their endless, bloody verbal procrastination, their "listening to each other" and hearing what each other says. I try really hard to be patient, and to <u>listen</u>, to what they're saying and to enter lovingly into their dreams and confusions. But both these latter are so often so unrealistic that I can see the whole project bumbling on forever and never being done and <u>that</u> makes me despair. The project itself excites me, at its best, it could be a Life Center a la (your husband's) dreams.

✳

We are preparing for a Spring Fair to raise funds for the school. Our house looks like a rag shop, with various crafty projects being undertaken in separate corners — I have ones that I can pick up and put down, ones I have to concentrate on, all set up all over the house, so that when the appropriate time/space happens, I can avail myself of the opportunity without having to get it all up. However, this does mean we eat with blanket fluff on the table occasionally and also do a fair bit of stepping over and around. Still, we <u>have</u> to make this successful; the school needs money badly, and if it's a good day, the possibility of making quite a lot seems fairly reasonable.

*

Headache all day and so I felt the sadness in me more than usual — the sadness of leaving this place, this life and the people I love. The weekend has been full of the 'best' of this community — my birthday, the parents' festival in the new hall, the international evening at the college, a good meeting — and clear, sunny, crisp autumn days — with light pulling out the golds and greens and browns of all the fields and trees and hedgerows. When I really let myself think of leaving, I wonder how I will bear it. How can I say good-bye? And still I think we should, and will go.

*

Your move to Detroit sounds so many things. Exciting, scary — it will surely be different to Forest Row. Baptism by Fire. I'm sure that wherever you go, whenever, you'll find a task. Even from this short distance, I can see a pattern in our various moves — as always, there <u>is</u> a consistent thread

— the thread in the labyrinth — follow it long enough and you find your way out! — running through it all, though it's only now I begin to see what it is — I am still far from knowing where it will lead. Wherever, it seems clear to me that the point is that you get on with whatever fate throws in front of your nose, until the pattern is clear enough for you to grasp the wheel and steer the direction for yourself.

✳

Why is it always even later to bed when my husband is away? And I still start new projects at 11:00 — crazy! But I like the peace of nighttime — peace in me and around me.

✳

I'm glad we've come to Holland. I love the flat open land, the huge sky, the pretty houses and all the water. The Dutch seem good at beautifying and humanizing their surroundings. Being here, I feel closer to all the Dutch people I have known. I think going to different countries does that — extends one's soul to that area of the world. Well, that's nothing new, but I've been aware of that here. Also, how being at Emerson, meeting so many people from so many different countries does that — takes you, connects you with all those different places and different ways of seeing and being.

✳

So much consciousness is required even to hear what someone like Rudolf Steiner has investigated — and somehow we must do our own work, in the ways we know how and with the capacities we have.

✳

Are you still acquiring possessions? I know well the mentality that goes with it. Whenever we are painting the house, etc. we find we spend our evenings discussing what color would be best, should we buy that new wastebasket or lampshade, or? — until my husband says something like "I can't believe you were ever a hippy" — or "what would your hippy friends think of you now? And then I try to defend myself. And on and on. But it's worth it in the end — and a necessary part of life.

✳

A friend is going to write us an article about Fat as a feminist issue for the newsletter. She's excited about it and has even started a group about it. Certainly seemed relevant to me this morning, as I tried to get into a pair of trousers that is suddenly too small. I'm sure if we were on the telephone, or going to Brighton, we could spend an hour on this depressing subject, but I'll restrain myself now and go have another piece of licorice to encourage me in my housework!

✳

The autumn was a terrible time for many people here: illness, marriage break-ups, nervous breakdowns, and a very tragic suicide. He leaves a wife and children of 6, 4 and 2. Also several people seemed to have car accidents.

✳

Oh, the endless levels of things. Sometimes I think I could be happy with just one — why can't life be simple? Of course, deeply and truly I know that meaning and life arise out of, in between all those levels — but maybe my mother brought me up to seek for happiness and simplicity, so sometimes I long to go to sleep.

✳

The house is in chaos, and we intend our annual spring cleaning, yet I wonder where the energy will come from. I don't feel like cleaning house. I think by the time I am a little old lady I will be living in a messy house. And as long as my friends still visit me, I don't care. I think for me it might be the right progression — or is that just a justification for my gradual but growing laziness in that area?

What I want to do and will do is to curl up with Saul Bellow's new novel — *The Dean's December*. I actually spent £8 on it as soon as I knew it was out, and it's like meeting an old friend after seven or so years. So warm and familiar. Of course it's possible I won't like it, but I doubt it. There is something about him, his work that hooks up to a central thread in my life and development. And there's nothing like a good novel to make me feel and know it's holiday time.

✳

A sad and difficult thing — (The children were playing with a neighbor child who said) "her mommy had made one condition on the sale of their house, that the people were Christian and that they would never send their children to the local Waldorf school." It really saddened me and bothered me. The kids haven't played together since and I have been reluctant to make any further arrangements, although their play was fine, and on the surface the parents seemed friendly. But for me it called to mind Hitler, and people not selling their houses to blacks, and the other kinds of prejudice and hatred that is sown from such tiny seeds as that. Maybe my reaction was extreme, but I felt shocked and troubled by it. It somehow took it beyond the realm of freedom where you can differ but respect, or anyway accept a particular and different path for another.

✳

Someone asked a lecturer at a conference how or what we could/can/should do to understand and face the end of the 20th century. Where can we find help? He said: Contact Tycho de Brahe! Naturally, he was asked to expand on that but never really did, except to speak about what Steiner says of him in the Karma lectures. Well, I thought contacting Tycho seemed too far away from where I was, but then I got into one of my serious and slightly fearful thinks about the end of the century — sparked off by watching children <u>at the seaside</u> playing computer games and space invaders, etc. by the hour and seeing their faces and worrying about my lovely innocents in this strange and ever stranger world. So I decided if I read Koestler's *Sleepwalkers*, I could make some effort towards a contact and maybe that would help me prepare and have right thoughts, etc. I realize the comical side of me trying to contact Tycho de Brahe, but when you're desperate you overcome your prejudices and inhibitions and will try all and everything.

✳

I read the Salomé book you sent. It was good but I wasn't totally convinced by her. I found it more interesting for the picture of the time, and of Rilke, Nietzsche and others. Do you think she was a free spirit — or just in love with herself? Was she creative herself or is she famous for inspiring famous men? I'm not really sure what I think.

✳

Ever-recurring questions and thoughts on family festivals and celebrations

I feel such a need to renew my whole relation to Advent and Christmas. I felt it last year but didn't do it, and although it was fine in the end, I don't think I can continue to ride on past energy. (My husband) suggested we find a new plot to the story, a new story — helpful as always!

*

1983 – 1985

I realize more and more that without the children's participation, enthusiasm and innocence, without, too, all the old rituals we have built up and which become a bit empty now, I don't know what to do. It's part of my facing a real crisis, lack of rhythm in a deeper sense. Something I've always thought I wasn't <u>too</u> bad at really, I find now without the children's needs dictating a form to me, I am at a loss.

*

Yesterday afternoon I had a long luxurious talk with a visiting teacher, and I realized how <u>hardly ever</u> do I just sit and talk with people without some particular aim or purpose. I realized I do that even less with people of my generation. Should that not be important? For me, shoulds or not, I realize it is. Because I think maybe there is something new our generation needs, is bringing up, but how can we ever really know it, find it, work consciously with it if we don't talk with each other? I'm usually working here — especially now that you and your husband have gone—with people older and wiser and what a gift that is, I know. But still, I do miss the forging together personally and professionally that we had and that maybe in a very special way we can have with others the same ages.

*

I need a housewife. How do you sort out priorities when there are too many interwoven ones?

*

A hospital ward is an interesting form of community — from what I have observed so far, very quick bonding takes place based on complete sharing of symptoms and suffering and the giving of sympathy and support to the other. All the surface, the masks are let down, and you meet quickly the humanity in the other and the indignity of large souls and spirits caught in physical bodies that have to be poked and prodded with instruments of various kinds.

*

Ah, how easy it is to plan books from one's bedside, when one—me!—has no energy even to make the bed!

The frustrating thing is, I feel I have a lot of energy and enthusiasm for thinking and doing things — but suddenly it's gone underground or blown away, or in hibernation or something — fire turned to water. Well it's hard to describe this terrible exhaustion. Hard to accept too.

＊

The Peace Conference gets closer. I wonder what I'll do. I'd really rather be participating. If you have done some new and successful exercises to do with the masculine and feminine, or the feminine, or relationships, could you please — soon — write them down for me and send them. I want each day to have some kind of artistic exercise. Otherwise, there will be too much talking.

＊

I'm trying to wade through Germaine Greer's new book — *Sex and Destiny*. Have you read it? It's strange — a lot I agree with, a lot I think is provocative and good food for thought, but I find it very disturbing too. And as always I find that such a subject, taken on without a spiritual view of the human being, leaves many gaps and questions, and I wonder in the end what the effect is. It's not exactly light reading, but I am rather lightly reading it.

＊

The Peace Conference was very exciting and very worth

the effort. I felt very involved in the organization from the beginning, and then I had two groups — three days each. I realized again how important and alive questions on the Feminine and related themes still are, yet in different ways than in the '70's. Many things have been worked through, but new depths and areas continue to emerge. It was especially exciting for me to put all our work in a new context. I found that it was the exercises, observations, artistic experiences of the theme that led to the deepest experiences and conversations, and brought the groups together. The first three days, we looked mostly at Feminine and Masculine and modern imaginations of the Feminine, and how that is related to our work for peace. The second three days, we focused on relationships and peace. They were the most inspiring groups, with the most awake and articulate people I've had for years. There were lots of men in the groups too, which was good. Many of the people had really worked inwardly and outwardly on the questions. A number were connected with Anthroposophy but most not, although all were searching and many were very active in the current Green/Peace Movement. I came away from the week exhausted, but very inspired and excited.

*

Have you had much contact with the Peace/Green Movement there? I wish I could share properly with you. — how important and exciting I found our reaching out into that movement this summer — personally and also for

Emerson and Anthroposophy in England. It was an important step — a breathing out and making links to other searching, spiritually striving and awake people. I love it and think we must take it further next year.

*

One of the reasons for my time problems the last couple of weeks is that I happened to start reading a two volume autobiography by Eugenia Ginzburg — *Into the Whirlwind* and *Within the Whirlwind* about her 18 years in prison, solitary confinement and labor camp during the Stalin 'reign of terror,' after being falsely accused of terrorism. It is an incredibly beautiful story of unimaginable suffering and courage and humanity. Also of a woman. You would love it.

*

I never see my friends — or if I do it's a snatched five minutes where all we have time for is to express a hunger for a real conversation — sometime. We have very little social life — none really.

*

People mutter about the destroyed ozone, the French nuclear tests in the Pacific, Halley's Comet. I wonder where it will all end, and how it will all end and when it will all end. Sometimes I feel as though I can almost grasp some sort of evolution; some sort of purposeful destruction of what is now, to get somewhere else. Sometimes. Other times it seems far more random, out of our control, more unconscious than any of that. And it's hard not to think about what faces these children — I don't mean just mine. I mean all of them, any of them.

✳

Thank you so much for the prints on Childhood to Old Age by Thomas Cole. They really are beautiful in how they capture the growing through life. I long for a time soon to look at them more closely. Of course I identify with 'Manhood,' as it's called — the poor fellow tense, beseeching, heading for the rapids with the angel far behind him and some pretty angry-looking beings hovering above — not to mention the dark tormented landscape!

✳

I suppose the main trouble with my — our? — lives is there is so little time, even for seeing the people we love. And yet, in the end, what is more important?

CHAPTER 2

Mothers and Children

Many of my letter-writing friends were mothers, some already when we met and others as the years went by. The different reflections on motherhood are funny, moving, sometimes conflicted, and also permeated with the sense that our responsibility as mothers was something to be taken seriously. Most of the mothers quoted here were to some extent, at least theoretically, sharing parenting responsibilities with a partner, but there were also single mothers bravely trying to make life work for themselves and their children. Among my friends who did not yet have children, some were not sure if they wanted to. For others, a first or later, pregnancy brought unexpected challenges. A miscarriage also elicited surprising reflections.

When these letters were written, beginning in 1973, both childcare and part-time work were often difficult for women to find. This began to change over the years, and some of the letters address the developing challenge of juggling family and work responsibilities. Now in the 21st century, in many parts of the world, mothers have no choice but to work outside the home, even if they might wish to stay home with their young children. Often mothers take only a few weeks of maternity leave before returning to demanding careers. The letters reflect a time of transition for women in terms of economic realities, personal ambition, childcare possibilities, and work opportunities for mothers.

As stated in the last chapter, many of the writers were actively considering the idea of reincarnation, the possibility that we come into a life that is not completely arbitrary, but rather rich with unconscious intentions —perhaps one could call them invitations — for further development toward becoming an ever more whole human being. Connected to this were questions about the meaning of being a mother, the learning being offered toward our own development and more broadly at this time in history when women's roles and possibilities, choices and challenges were in such transition. It is noteworthy that even in some of the recordings of things the writers' children said, there is an innate sense for repeated earth lives in the young child's own perceptions of life.

I have rather arbitrarily separated this chapter into two parts — comments and questions about being a mother, and then descriptions by mothers of their children at various ages.

Motherhood
1973 – 1975

I have been sitting here sort of fuming after my latest — about the 100th — encounter with a total stranger — even over the phone — who felt the necessity and the right to express the opinion that "really two is too young to leave a child." You'd think I were leaving him on a doorstep when all I asked this woman was if she might be able to watch him one morning — 3 hours — a week. I am so tired of receiving dogmatic statements about what I should and shouldn't do — by people who don't know me or my children. Everyone has something to say about the situation — and I've received threats of the most dire consequences — future psychological disturbances, bedwetting, you name it! I understand what stands behind a lot of what people are saying, and I feel that 'the Mother' is important, but people are so locked in rigid images. The way I have my schedule worked out I need to be away from the kids for 15 hours a week.

I am with the younger one part of all but two mornings and with him all of one, and every afternoon with both of them. And they are doing all right! A lot of people here are really unprogressive — to say the least! They are either heavy on theory but never have been near a child, frustrated mothers who don't want anyone else to have it 'better,' plain out-and-out male chauvinists, and so on. I don't mean to be so critical but people keep pushing me into a very defensive corner — or trying to.

*

How to see 'Motherhood' as a phase of one's life — and a phase that can be full of development? The old attitudes must be totally transformed for acceptance by a struggling, self-conscious, ever-questioning populace that is still steeped in peer pressures of prestige and worth.

*

If you aren't sitting down, I suggest that you do because I have an even bigger bombshell. I am pregnant. Needless to say, it wasn't planned. I can't believe how ironic it all is — both in terms of my own plans and desires, but also when I got your letter last week saying you had been wanting to have a baby for a few weeks! It's the last thing I wanted — I'm sorry it couldn't have worked out the other way.

*

Actually it really is all very difficult to figure out and deal with. Plus there is a strong chance of miscarriage because of the IUD, and I don't want that to happen. When one thinks of it in terms of a soul wanting to incarnate, it just gets all the more complicated. It is so hard for me to deal with the reality of another baby and all the ramifications of that, when there is still such uncertainty about whether it will make it. I have felt pretty awful for the last 10 days or so, but I am trying to rest more now. There is so much and yet so little to say about all of this. We really just have to wait and see how the next few months go. And I have to begin again to re-assess my whole picture of myself and my future. I have to slow down again and try to figure out what it all means.

*

I find increasingly that within the role of 'motherhood' there is great opportunity for development and growth — if only one can overcome the subtle 'modern' pressures of one's peers and oneself, and instead be truly open to what is happening with one's children and the world they and you experience. But it's still hard! And then I tell myself that there will be other phases to my life!

*

My courses are quite interesting and very good in terms of making me really want to get busy developing myself a little. — I had to insert the 'want to' because I certainly haven't actually been getting anywhere. Unfortunately, I haven't really gotten to know anyone because I am always running out of my classes to be with the children. I don't mean unfortunately in terms of being with the children because that is very important to me, but just that it would be nice to really be able to meet some people. Even as it is, I am worried about the children and may just drop it all.

*

I'm in one of those crummy moods where you just want to go drop in on someone you like so you don't have to directly entertain yourself — or in this case, the children. But there is no one for us to visit. Neither of the children napped today, and they are whiney and crabby and I'm tired too and don't feel like playing with them. My husband won't be home for two more hours, so here I sit — trying to tell myself to rise above it! — with little success. So while the kids are in the yard temporarily amusing themselves, I'll try to write you a note. Don't mind my complaining please — I feel better just expressing to someone.

*

I'm experiencing the problem of *thinking* with small children — no concentrated time to read, think, converse.

Everyday I'm trying to find something good that happened, something positive, a thought I liked today. Even one sentence to build observation and perspective.

＊

Did I tell you that we spoke with an acquaintance after the miscarriage? He said that there are many souls who cannot bear to actually incarnate into the world as it is now, but who need to come down a little — to develop some strength for some later incarnation. He gave as an example, someone who lived a very spiritually developed but physically protected life last time — i.e. in a monastery or convent in the 14th or 15th centuries — and now they just can't stand to come into our hardened world, but they must have some contact with it. There is presumably a strong connection with the family and especially the mother — this connection can last a long time or fade out after the miscarriage. He said also that sometimes the soul gives something to the family through the whole experience. In a way, we really felt this after the miscarriage — we suffered a lot through it all, but afterward we both felt we had grown and been given a great deal — individually and together.

＊

A friend spoke to me about my mothering: she feels as if I am seeing my children for the first time when I see them — as if they were precious jewels. I can feel this too, although

I had never thought of it. Sometimes I see them and I have to enjoy — love — them, not because they belong to me in any sense, but because they are the ways they are.

＊

1976 – 1978

How to find 'perspective' for a mother with a young child who despairs about all she is missing? Question of a woman being 'under water' with young children — this in relation to the fact that she 'is waiting' for some future time when other parts of her can develop. Is this asked of us by others — husband, children — or do we in fact ask it of ourselves? One 'resigns' oneself to it knowing that the tension of not entering into either realm (mother/wife or developing/working person) is too great. From this entering in, one of course does/can develop — by living with reality. Still, the struggle of not wanting to be totally underwater. The level at which we talk of 'waiting' and our sense of relationship is quite different from other people we know — i.e. a friend relating of her partner, at each move saying, "You have two choices: come with me or get a divorce."

＊

What is the experience of motherhood — through the traumas and the loneliness, what can be given, developed, and also lost — positive and negative? How much of this can — must? — be developed if one is not a mother? — i.e. in other spheres of life/ work, as a task, the gift of the feminine — nurturing, warmth, caring, protecting.

I fear some want easy formulas for balance — but balance *is* tension, growth *is* struggle, consciousness *is* choices. Can one do everything well simultaneously?? What does this really mean?

*

Is the pain of decision-making the problem of our generation of women? We *must* be conscious — but it's so hard in the consequences — we can't just fall back. But can we be clear of the 'agreements' — responsibilities we make, or choose to make? — i.e. to have or not to have a child — take *responsibility* — in the widest sense for this decision.

*

A friend asked us about (our) having a child, and we talked about it on the way home, and decided, among other things, that the only way we could realistically have a child is if we also had a full-time maid or housekeeper. I am such a terrible housewife, I don't think we'd make it otherwise. The other aspect is that my husband said he is getting too old to make a 20 year commitment to a child. Realistically, I'm not sure I am emotionally capable of taking good care of a child. And then if we don't have a child, I'm not sure that that is what I want. And I wonder if I am being subtly influenced by my socialization process that says it is a woman's 'duty' to have children. I don't think that, in my case, the socialization of being a 'typical female' has been that strong, yet I'm not sure, and I don't know whether part of my ambiguous motivation to have a child is based on guilt feelings stemming from the socialization process. I just don't know. Sometimes I think it would be marvelous not to have a child, and other times I recognize that if I am not going to be famous (in my field of work), then maybe I should have a child, I suppose as doing something unique. And I guess that really should not be the motivation of having a child. All in all, it is a very difficult question. I also think I should come to a decision about it, and not let the decision be made for me by default, which would be the coward's way out. Do you have any thoughts on the subject? It is a personal decision, but all the help counts!!!

✳

Motherhood has been a central theme in my *experience*. It was not a question before it was a reality — it came in with a very real sense of the responsibility of motherhood. I felt early resentment and anxiety, but knew the responsibility was real. If the twenties are a time of struggling for an 'adult' sense of self as an individuality, the situation for this *for me* was as a wife and mother. I felt a constant struggle for the balance of responsibility that is real to others, and the responsibility that must also to be real to myself. Therefore I had questions of why be a woman, why a wife, why a mother — i.e. what real 'self' did/do I intend to be responsible to? — not the cultural, P.R., 'liberated' self of theories, nor some 'traditional' non-self — but really what does my 'being' intend to do?

My toddler is sitting on my knee which will probably make this impossible. Oh for two hours of free time to sit, to be with you, even if over this distance. If I'm not careful, this letter will end up sounding incredibly negative. I'm in one of those — fortunately fairly rare — victimized resentful moods, when I want relief (from my child). It's funny — there's only one person I can feel resentful towards, and that's my husband, and I know HEADWISE that that is completely unfair. What little 'free' time he has, he spends on the garden or chores, or building things for us both, and I feel badly subtracting from such essentials. But it would be useless for me to deny that there are times or some days when I have HAD IT — it would be <u>glorious</u> to be able to say to someone — anyone — please take her for just an hour — even if I just went and sat and felt guilty for doing nothing!

About her two small boys
The more I have some time for myself — Monday and Wednesday afternoon I have a paid babysitter — the more I enjoy being with them and doing things with them.

*

The reason I put pen to paper in such untimely haste now — it being a mere six weeks or so since my last letter — is to tell you that I am, indeed, pregnant. I have mixed feelings in unveiling my bulge-to-be. Of course, I'm pleased, and so is my husband. And really, I must say I feel almost like a pawn in the whole thing — and I write that fully aware of the dangers and consequences of the illusions of resigned responsibility. But I swear, I feel I had almost no choice. So, in a way, it feels very right, that I should be pregnant. And I can look forward happily to the thought of another child, for I do find this motherhood an amazingly learning and growing time and — at the moment, at least — an enjoyable and not too dementing one. <u>But</u>, I'm sorry there'll be 2½ years between this child and the second one. The first two are so close, and so much a unit, play really well together — I almost can't believe it. So I don't know if I expect you to, but they really <u>love</u> each other. I keep thinking it will probably change when the second becomes more of an ego, as undoubtedly much of the love of the relationship is set by the first, who is so gentle and generous towards the second that it just boggles me. But at the moment, and for the last six months or so, they are a joy to watch together, I worry that this child will be, or feel, an appendage to them. And even though I know it's futile to wonder about that, I do. Also, I'm sorry that it will be effectively, another five or six years yet before I'm free to pursue any child-unencumbered activities. Even though I am aware of many parts of my being growing and changing through these children, I'm also aware of parts of me that are never watered these days, and though I know they'll lie there, dormant, until another time comes for them, I feel, at times, the lack of their dimension.

*

1979 – 1981

Could I really be pregnant? The question rarely leaves my mind — it seems so unlikely, and yet there are the symptoms. I wish I knew, one way or the other. The waiting in uncertainty is worst of all. What is this for me? What must I learn that I obviously haven't yet?

A part of me is so happy working, feeling a part of the staff preparing for the new students. And another part despairs at maybe losing this — quiet confusion perhaps is better than despair — why? It's hard to understand — and live with in a good way.

*

A lot of the time I feel like a really lousy mother, and because I don't like to feel I'm less than — at least — magnificent at anything, I don't enjoy the sensation. I hear myself say things that I think are absolute crap, and ½ of me says, "How <u>could</u> you!" The other ½ says, "You *deserved* that, you little rotter!" Ah well, the joys of parenting. I look at (the baby), so innocent and emanating nothing except well being and peace and I think — to think you'll be like this (older sibling) in four years time — that I <u>know</u> it! Still that very perspective of where he'll be and what he'll be doing in one, six and twelve months hence, makes him <u>very</u> enjoyable. It's taken me til this child to really obtain this perspective, and it does alter my consciousness of present moments — both good and bad. And I can intellectually at least, apply this known perspective to (my daughter). All things must pass...

✳

The children had colds all week and were home from school — in turn. I feel how packed my life is — when one pin comes out, there is a general collapse. I just rush from thing to thing — hardly breathing and always feeling bad about what I'm <u>not</u> doing — hard then to be <u>in</u> what I am doing. This 'working mother' life is difficult. I want it but there are such inevitable complications — and I'm lucky, (my husband) will now try to help/be here when he can. I feel for mothers alone with small children and full time jobs. A part of me would love to just collapse with the kids — totally <u>be</u> with them and not worry about all that isn't getting done.

I Give You My Word

＊

As usual, I've become my recalcitrant pregnant self — I have really to force myself to contact people when I'm pregnant, and often don't bother. Because (the older children) exist, I have to make some effort to find them other children to play with and this of course involves other women, but I find I'm such a vegetable that I just want to go away. I know, now, from experience, how differently I feel when I'm not pregnant, but that's no consolation when at the moment I am and feel it.

＊

I <u>do</u> find time in amongst all this frenetic outside work to be, to <u>really</u> be, with the kids and with (my husband). It's a constant struggle and one that really is a picture of my life — that inner-outer pull. Wanting to do everything well, but also wanting/needing acknowledgement — and you sure don't get that from raising kids. The children themselves have a chorus which goes — "She's an old witch, isn't she. We don't like <u>her</u>. We like Dad, don't we. He's a nice Poppa. We have a horrible mother, she smells!" The ultimate threat is "I'll bite your bed!" — !!!!?? Meanwhile (the baby) sits gazing adoringly at me, love pouring in a mutual stream from each little eyeball and all I can think is — "How long will it be before you, too, are telling me what a fiend I am?" (The oldest — age 5) said to me the other day, as I was working on this doll's house I'm making for them, "I wish we didn't have a mother who <u>made</u> things. I wish you weren't a <u>maker</u>." — I wish they didn't, too. I'd love all that time to be doing things for myself! She has recently been impossible in about every way imaginable. . . . She is incredibly moody/funny/bad tempered/prima donna-ish/obliging/engaging/impossible!

*

And into this comes another child! (4th) If I just believed she'd sleep! (My second child) didn't very well — though compared to (the third), she was nothing to complain about . . . so really, we've only had one good sleeper out of three — not a very consoling record! Hard not to look to oneself. I really don't understand <u>why</u> I have to have another child! I think that's the part I find hardest. . . . I mean, that, and the fact that we were contracepting to the point of paranoia. I know it will all make sense in five years time, but right now, <u>that</u> is cold comfort. The only sense I can make out of the whole thing is it's the only really appropriate crucifix I can think of and this seems relevant enough to my 33rd year. I <u>do</u> feel welcoming enough in my <u>heart</u> — but that's a congenital disease with me — I'll probably still be able to welcome my twelfth child in my <u>heart</u> — Oh well!

*

1982 – 1986

How/why can this small child phase of my life be going on so long? I wonder if it's because I can never learn anything unless I <u>really</u> learn it — two children is over so quickly — I can't believe you're only 36 and have a teenager — so much time left for you to do other things. I'll be ninety before this brood is out of the way and I already feel numb from the waist up 80% of the time! None of this is complaint — It's slightly bewildered wondering. What else can I do apart from raise children? As well as? Time will tell! I keep noticing my tendency to relish details of women who have had four or more children and still have managed to 'do something' in the world! The only thing that bothers me is they are almost always rich, as well.

*

I do feel I am going to have to make slightly more space in my life again for family — well really for teenagers for the next four years or so. I don't want to retreat from work that is needed and work in which I feel I have something to offer, but I don't want to be absent from (the children's) life when they need my attention. It's only a short time — and it means not so much cutting out daytime work as the endless nighttime work — meetings and evening preparing.

Some meetings will have to go and my preparing will have to fit into day times.

＊

I am about to write a sequel to *Lifeways* (*Lifeways — Working with Family Questions;* Ed. Gudrun Davy & Bons Voors, Hawthorn Press, 1983) called "The Good Enough Mothers' Club." I have so much to say on this subject that is wrenching my heart at the moment, that I want to talk to you, not write it. I have just watched a woman here, who in the name of MegaMother of the Epoch, has had four children in five years, has become a total recluse — "it's not good for your children to go in cars, under florescent lights, hear music, breathe petrol fumes, live, laugh, or have fun" — is a physical, and I suspect mental wreck, and whose only pleasure and glory seems to be that she's 'doing everything right.' So, the Good Enough Mothers' Club will be born, and members are allowed to work, allowed even, to take their children to the local swimming pool for a dose of chlorine every now and again. They can shop, swear, cry, eat take-away food when the occasion demands it — like the night before their period is due — they can buy birthday presents and shop-made Christmas decorations. In short, they, too, can have fun in what little time is left to them after the rigors of <u>normal</u> motherhood, without contributing to the pressure by making everything themselves. I have taken to such bizarre comments as "nothing is homemade in this house except the babies," which of course isn't true, but (people) keep trying to outdo each other with who is doing it really 'rightest' of all. It's enough to make me start buying bread and jam, which I haven't done ever in my life — in fact, at this moment I am making my 35th jar of cumquat marmalade for this morning. You've got to keep laughing I guess, I would more, if it didn't have such an insidious effect on the whole community. Even if other people don't do it, they feel guilty.

It scares me that I so often seem so abstracted — <u>am</u> so abstracted — am only half listening to (the children) as I think of what the next (work question needs), or how we can possibly solve this, this, or this... Maybe I'm a bad mother. I can't tell. I find it so hard to know. The kids seem ok most of the time. They certainly <u>seem</u> to be the things I think I want them to be, at least <u>some</u> of the time. And if they manage that, then perhaps it doesn't matter that I'm always busy, often crabby and only ½ listening? Or am I really just a failure? I badly want to go to a conference in August and it makes me ask so many questions about me and motherhood and (work) and they're all hard ones to answer! Maybe I've just got impossibly high standards? Maybe they are the only kind to have? Maybe it's good for them all to realize they <u>do</u>

miss me? Or is it absolutely devastating for a child not to think they are categorically <u>the</u> most important thing in a mother's life? Are my children that? I don't even know what <u>is</u> the most important — I guess they are — should they be? And on it goes — a piece of my mind, or no peace of mind. But never mind!

*

Can you remember what it's like? We haven't been away alone since they were born! We hardly ever even get a night in bed alone! And I am on call 24 hours per day — there is never any time to accomplish anything and always constant interruptions and necessities. But of course, it's also <u>very</u> wonderful. I really can't think of any more special 'vocation,' and my life would be very empty indeed without them. Some form of part-time work or 'self-employment' helps to link me to the 'outside' world, I've found.

*

(The new baby) is now lying on the bed giggling. She is so old-looking. I am totally exhausted — I sleep max 5 hours and go flat out all day. But I am happier than I've ever been. I suppose that I'm not searching and that long quest of mine is what really exhausts me — it exhausts my spirit. At the moment my spirit is at peace — bliss.

*

Images of Children

Throughout the letters are many expressions of longing that the reader will know the writer's children. There are efforts to share special moments, experiences of wonder or frustration, and the endearing ways of being of a particular child. These excerpts are full of the joy, confusion, and challenge that our children bring to us. Instead of arranging this section chronologically as the letters were written, but rather to follow images of development from baby to teenager, I have grouped the different passages roughly according to the ages of the children being described.

I firmly believe in my super-optimistic way, that by the time — WHEN? — we're (back home) and letters are <u>really necessary</u>, I <u>will</u> have time to write — by then (the baby) will of course be sleeping all those hours she's clocking up now — I'm keeping tally of all the hours she's awake, when she <u>should</u> be asleep, and I'm going to make her sleep them off at certain convenient strategic points in our life. And who am I kidding? Enough — I <u>refuse</u> to talk about her — it's morning, by the way, and she is — dare I breathe the word — 'as_ _ _ p'. I have this developing theory — to take the place of all my others on children and child rearing which have fallen like flies — that we have thought transference — every time I think anything about her, she stirs, and usually wakes up and so I am 'conditioning' my mind to stay free while she's not awake.

. . .

However, though we appear to have passed out of the unburpable stage — did I say I wasn't going to discuss her? — and onto one far worse — I wonder if this is how it goes, everything is the worst at the time. It's only in retrospect when something even worse is happening, that you realize the former state wasn't in fact too bad. I suspect this culminates in the grandiose and fearful time called Adolescence — you've heard about it maybe? — You have 7-8 years to go, baby, so start preparing yourself.

✳

It has been beautiful, these last three weeks, to watch (my husband) really beginning to play with (the baby). He's had plenty of opportunity. He is really funny — and she just laughs and smiles all the time he is with her. He takes your red gnome, which we've temporarily christened Fredigar Bolger (from Lord of the Rings) and walks him up and down all over her in the baby sitter and she just dies — curls up with smiles. She is also beginning to be fascinated by his beard — or what's left of it — she yanks at it so hard that it comes out. We've christened her Blink-ogg, which is bright-eyes in Afrikaans — she doesn't miss a thing.

(My third child) is beautiful. He is bigger at four months than the girls were at 13 months. They were exceptionally small — he is normal. Very bonny and <u>so</u> friendly. He's a really placid, happy child. He's sitting up already. He's <u>so</u> pleased with himself, permanently. (His sisters) are still very accepting of his presence. I hear (the second one) talking to him, repeating all the things <u>we</u> say, and it sounds so dear. Because I'm so much better at all this babying, now that I've had more practice, I'd like to go on. I mean, it seems pointless to stop, once you finally know how to do it. But I look at (the oldest), who is very much a CHILD, not a baby — and I don't want to have to deal with <u>that</u> over and over. Even assuming that I'll get better at it too, I'm sure it'll still be painful. I'm considering radical contraception. Will dither and dally, no doubt; probably till I no longer need worry about contraception! What a pain in the arse consciousness is.

*

(The baby) is very easy to manage, now, but was anything but that from 4–5 weeks till she was 4 months. In fact, I was quite often really frantic in that time. She cried almost non-stop every minute she was awake, and it was awful. She was awake a lot. I have no idea <u>what</u> was wrong. By now, of course, I have to work quite hard even to remember it happened, and how it was, which I guess is the good thing about bad times with children — they just don't count.

※

I wish you could see her. God — more than I can ever tell you. Teeth everywhere, and she has this crazy squinty smile at the moment which displays their crooked glory magnificently. I want so much for you to be able to share her — and yet words seem so inadequate, so one-dimensional and somehow describing a state past when she is such a state present — flowering. All babies must be — they change so quickly. I see such a 'first childness' in her — she is very independent and 'alone' — can't explain the latter much more than that. She barely tolerates cuddles from us and I try not to push it. But I refuse to give in entirely. She will sometimes, very rarely, snuggle into one or the other of us, but mostly holds herself stiffly backwards, preferring to bestow her affections from a distance and by such gestures as giving you pieces of half chewed toast or apple.

I am always amazed — I mean, daily surprised by how much she understands. The other day, I was hunting for her shoes — of which she is inordinately proud — and conducting a running commentary: "Where are your shoes?..." Next thing, she came crawling over, one in each hand and I freaked! I had no idea she understood so much. That's one example of many, lately. Very sensitive to my moods too — and I try to keep myself even, if for this reason alone.

❋

She has *so* many words now and says them all the time, often irrespective of appropriateness. Children show me so much of myself — and this child, with such day-to-day contact — I decide 90 times a day I *must* stop this or that — I hear my tones of voice. She automatically crushes and smells *all* leaves, grass she picks. I couldn't work out why til I realized I'm always doing it in the herb garden. And last week, on two separate occasions, she saw a piece of marjoram and a piece of thyme lying on the table and said, "Herb, Herb!" (Or her, her) I cannot believe how much she knows, does this fucking just grow, I wonder? She is very manipulative — neither of us deals well with it — and so conscious of herself.

❋

(My toddler) was so dear feeding the ducks. He wanted to get right by them and touch them so he would run eagerly up — scaring them of course. As they scattered from him he looked so hurt — and would try again offering cookies. When they would eat the cookies he would beam. He tried their quacking and their walking and was totally absorbed.

❋

(My two year old) is really talking. Sentences everywhere. I <u>love</u> her words and word order. I get such <u>pleasure</u> when she says a word well, after struggling for a couple of days, it's unreal. I could hug her each time. She won't let me. She talks non-stop, to me, to (her baby sibling), to her 'family' — a conglomerate of dolls, bear, dog, and sundry temporary favorites — all day. "Don't move baby" — I hear myself. The other day I heard "I can't stand it" and really felt bad — because I <u>know</u> I used to say that when (the baby) was going through her grim time and would wake up for the 10th time in two hours. She coined 'jamalade' the other day, which broke us up. I also love "motey-bike" and "cuppee tea." She sings "here we go round the Mouldy Bush" and "This is the wave we clean our teeth." She has the intonation and inflection <u>perfect.</u> It's so nice too that she is at a 'helping' stage — <u>loves</u> to set the table, carry parcels, feed cats, etc. — if only that sort of thing could last. She loves to go with (her father) to milk Bessie, and as usual is great on sound effects — from the plop plop plop of her shitting ½ way through milking to the pss pss pss of the milk going into the bucket. At the moment, her favorite book is the catalogue for a sale from a furniture store. She asks (her father) to 'read' it to her every night after supper. If, after the 5th time, his enthusiasm wanes and he says "last one," she says "Little more last one read it." See what I mean about word order. Her vocabulary includes 'impossible,' 'unlikely,' and lately, 'ridiculous' which is an interesting pointer to <u>my</u> conversations, I think — most of which are with myself.

*

(My son) was so funny today — he began talking real gibberish but with a slight intonation (of the language spoken where we are living). I looked over at him, he grinned and said, "That's the way some people talk Mommy — in the Laundromat!" And of course he was so right. I wonder what goes on in his little head — and what can another language mean to him?

*

(My three-year-old) is a dear boy — at times utterly angelic, and, no longer a baby. He takes everything in and surprises us with what he has observed. He adores (his sister), who runs his life as much as possible, but this year he has begun to assert his own rights and ways. Typical example: after a Christmas play (his six-year-old sister) kept asking and finally decided that the angel was not a real angel but a man dressed up. Finally, she said this and added, "Right?" (to her brother). He: "Yeah — and he flew down from heaven."

*

The other day (the three-year-old) was drawing — he really is just getting into recognizable forms, and he makes many pictures every day. This time he made a box house of sorts and in it put two long straight lines with a circle on top. He looked up at us with his wonderful grin and happily announced: "That's a growing boy." Of course — that's where he is — all things, like he, are in growth — big long limbs and the roundness of his being — never a thought of completion.

＊

The other day (my son and a friend — both three) were playing 'honey' and they decided to get married and have a baby. After much discussion about who should be the mommy, (my son) won out. At one point, I was in the room and they ran out giggling, saying "Let's leave, we don't want her to see our bosoms!" Then (my son) stuck a doll up his sweater and marched around pregnant — first they went to church to be married and then to the ambulance to have the baby!

＊

(My daughter) is gradually emerging from a positively hideous 3½ year-old stage, which was worse than her 2½ year-old stage, though reminiscent of same and which eclipsed the good times in between, and which made me wonder all over again how I can possibly have spawned such a fiend and how I dare repeat the performance. Just as she emerges and is really sweet, loving and flexible and accommodating and about everything I could wish for in a child of her age, (my second child) is preparing to enter 2½ with a bang. I can <u>see</u> it in the purse of her lips and the look in her eye. And I <u>know</u> hers will be everything as ghastly as (her sister's), but in such different ways that I'll still have to deal with it all over again — nothing like benefitting from experience.

*

(My older child) wants a "baby, a cat or a dog." (Her younger sibling) said he would be quite happy to settle for a cat! Then he thought we should have two babies, but in response to (his sister's) and my dismay announced most seriously, "That's all right, we could share the baby!"

*

The joy of the children in their new bicycles is phenomenal. (Our son) was totally absorbed and radiant. He refused to get off the trike in the shop, rode it down the sidewalk to the car, refused lunch and went most reluctantly to nap. He awoke and was immediately on it again! (Our daughter) on the other hand has been anticipating a 'training wheel bike' for over a year but when the day finally came, the excitement was interwoven with a tingling of fear. In her own cautious way she rather explored the bike before lunch, but only after nap let herself actually 'ride' — as she articulated it: "You don't feel so sort of nervous and afraid after you've had your lunch and nap and you even start to like it. Do you know that feeling Mommy?" She has many such statement/questions about feelings lately — always expressed in her thought-out, philosophical way.

✳

I wish you could see the children...[The oldest] is full of unanswerable questions these days, like "Why is night so long?" or "What makes your body move?" Except in her bossy moods — like mother, like... — she really is so dear. (The youngest) is a bumbling little steam roller who would appear at times to believe that might makes right! But then he will suddenly cuddle into my lap and murmur, "Mommy's little boy." He talks a great deal now and is at that point where he gets very angry at you when you don't understand him.

✳

(Our daughter) mastered her bike today — without the training wheels — and the excitement was incredible! Her whole body beamed. She rode laughing down the road — wobbling away — a funny juxtaposition of her intense and her scattered selves... When (my husband) took off the training wheels he said, "Well you won't be needing these anymore." She looked at him and said, "Well I won't be needing them in this life, but after I die and then come back again, I might need them again." There is a living concept of reincarnation — at a 5-year old level!

✳

(The five year old) is really so hearty and good natured and eager. We walked to the Market today and although we walked at least 2 miles in the windy cold, she never complained but took it all in with great interest. One of the sellers gave her a small cotton hankie and she talked for an hour about how lucky she was, and how did he know her dolly needed a new skirt, blouse, etc. She gets more complicated all the time — she has real moods now, and desires, and schemes, and thoughts and hurts.

✳

Must tell you about (my daughter) and the last pregnancy — about which she heard nothing from us. From — about — the day I was pregnant, she asked everyday — several times — about having a baby — when, how, who, etc, etc. The possibility, probability and desire for one were a part of her daily life — with joy and excitement. But since the day I began bleeding, she has not mentioned it again — never — not: can we have a baby? when? how soon? — nothing. I feel sure that she was connected to that soul, that she in some way was with it through its experience, and that she knew when it retreated… Also, Rosie — my renamed old teddy bear — was born during those days I was in bed and became a totally living and loved friend.

✳

The beauty of a little girl really moving into herself. So full of questions, opinions, philosophical thought. Still happy in her fantasy worlds and yet so often ready and astute in an adult world. We must keep her in balance — her quickness and intelligence must not overpower her, yet it must also not be pushed down. She is always so aware — "Sometimes I just forget all about what I'm doing, I get so interested in what grown-ups are saying."

✳

(This child) remains impervious in all directions. Are all 2nd children so lazy, amoral and guiltless?. . . But you know, she is still so easy to live with, such a joy to have around… The arbitrator still, she works hard at peace amongst these kids, and thinks of wonderful games to play. She has a wonderful catalyst quality… Amongst her peers this is also evident.

✳

(My six year old) is still so very innocent for all her seeming wisdom and quickness. She has such an alert and penetrating way, yet still things are wrapped in magic for her. We went to the Nutcracker and when it 'snowed' she seriously asked me if it was 'real' snow although we were close enough to 'see' that it wasn't. During the pause we went into the hall and could see out of the windows. She said: "Oh, no it wasn't real snow because it's not dark outside yet" — as it had been night in the show. Then later, at the end when Clara is back asleep and the Nutcracker is returned on her lap, she turned to me with eyes of wonder and said: "They must have two Nutcrackers, because the first one turned into a prince." I almost cried — she was so totally beautiful.

*

(Our daughter) really feels the specialness of having her bed by the window and she sees everything there with both great detail and great fantasy and love. She gestured to me about two branches that go this and that way and are two little ghosts — "I watch them all the time and they are mine."

Babies are still a big theme for both children. She wants to know — "really" — how and where they come from. She finally asked (her father) and when he said — ! — "ask your Mommy," she said, "Oh come on Daddy, you know. You can tell me!"

*

(The two boys) are playing a vile game which involves (the older one) using (the younger) as a variety of electrical appliances. It is a great favorite and I continue to withhold even a gritting of teeth, lest it encourage them. What fascinates me, is that these appliances and machines play virtually no part in their own lives, but they seek them out wherever they can, and investigate them ardently. And I don't suppose either of them will deign to be anything as mundane — or useful — as a washing machine mechanic.

*

I have to tell you what my dear daughter said to me as I bent down to kiss her tonight: "What are all those lines on your face — you know, around your mouth and stuff?" Nice, don't you think!? Nothing like being your own kid's 'aged mother.' Actually she was full of lovelies today. At dinner she said — after <u>much</u> consideration: "Mommy, I wouldn't trade you for 100 plastic toys" — pause — "and I <u>really</u> would like 100 plastic toys." I always say you can spot a Waldorf kid anywhere — they're the ones with the fastest grab at the plastic uglies!

*

A friend of mine is expecting a baby the end of June and (my six year old) said that "maybe Mommy's Daddy — who is dead — will come back as her baby!!" She talks about reincarnation quite often — completely from her own initiative.

*

(The children) and friends and dog have gone off through

the woods to be "pioneers" a la Laura Ingalls Wilder. Did you read those wonderful books as a child? The girls have put on their old-fashioned, ruffled dresses and (one boy) is complete with homemade bow and arrow. It is lovely to see them completely live into other times — it's amazing how much they really <u>become</u> their own characters — not acting in any self-conscious sense, but really entering into another consciousness.

This morning (my eight year-old son) asked me if I had ever dreamed about boys I had loved. I answered yes and then he asked me if I always knew them in real life or were some of them just in my dreams. I answered that some were just in my dreams and I didn't know them in real life. Then he told me that he had dreamed of a girl he loved but he didn't know her. I said maybe someday he would meet her. He looked so sad — as if he were going to cry and he just shook his head and said he hoped he dreamt of her again so he could finish his dream. I told him I hoped he could finish his dream, too.

Good evening with (our child's teacher) — he came out of concern for our moving and the possible effects on (the child) — and on the class here. He doesn't want it but listened warmly to us. He spoke of (this child) as a 'great soul' — needing still more protection — at least ideally. It's so hard to see what is best/right. I do worry about how it would all be for him.

*

(Our second child) is still as sanguine as ever a being was and as easy to have around as anyone could ever be. She amazes me! Just watching her take the little children in hand last night — play with them — selflessly, happily — and incidentally to their joy and delight — made me realize anew what a gift she is. She is a dear, dear child and long may she stay that way, though I'm sure she won't.

*

(8-year-old to his mother after visiting with cousins:) "Do you know what would happen if we had a TV? First we would just watch it some and then we would watch it more and more. And then after a while we would have a favorite rock star and we would have posters of him on our wall and we would start to dress like him . . . and then after a while we wouldn't be real anymore."

*

(My girl) is NINE — and one of the biggest mistakes I've made so far in my parenting is to prepare her for nine. In the six months or so pre-nine, when she would often break into tears over nothing, I spent lots of time giving her images for her coming sense of aloneness, etc. Now, when she is often being just an out and out bitch, and I chastise her, and point out how unfair or unkind she has been — usually to her brother, she says to me, "Well, what do you expect! Nine is a <u>difficult</u> age to be, you know."

I see her torn between love for me — with the intensity of the condemned, I think — and passionate contempt for me, which she is actually quite bewildered by. She is also about to begin with "Nobody loves me" — it happened once and made me aware of — remember — the depth to which one experiences that isolation. She has always liked beautiful things, but is easily persuaded about what <u>is</u> beautiful and what isn't — and in that sense can still be manipulated to be unaware. I see other tartlets in her class — all 8 or 9 — with purple feather earrings, punk hairstyles and their trendy clothes and am glad that it's still easy to avoid. Just to give her a little bit more space to grow unaware of all that super-physical stuff. God, I sound reactionary!!!

✳

I am filled with anxiety about tomorrow because (my child) is going on a cliff walk with a birthday party with... I dread to think how many lively little girls. It's <u>so</u> stormy and windy here and you can imagine my imagination keeps tracking familiar and not very fruitful paths — and off paths, over precipices. The words I was writing today about trusting the destiny of one's children — well, I keep saying them over to myself. Will I ever be free of this... it's better, but still I am caught and I never know what to do with it. Would I know a real premonition from a neurotic fantasy?

✳

(My child) is either experiencing the last of nine, or adolescence three/four years too early. I hope it's the former. She is like a mobile tantrum, waiting for a place to happen. Any excuse, <u>anything</u> will do, if she's in the right — wrong — mood. Alternate this with almost angelic helpfulness and sociability and a longing to be around me and talk to me when <u>I</u> least desire and require it, and you have the pretty picture of our current life.

✳

(My daughter) has grown up a lot this summer and says she already feels 10. She looks it, although in some ways she is still such a baby — in positive ways. But she seems less afraid of growing up, and I have worked to free myself of the desire to hold onto her baby sweetness and innocence.

✳

(About my 10½ year old) — If I try to think of the thing that is most revealing in our relationship at the moment, it must be the picture of her, sidling up to me, knowing not quite <u>what</u> she wants, but wanting me to know and to supply it. When I <u>don't</u> want to talk to her, talk with her, have her read over my shoulder, ask me what I'm doing, whom I'm about to ring, what I'm about to cook, etc. — she's <u>there</u> — and <u>mortally</u> offended if I suggest I might like a little space. But when <u>I</u> am free, available, wanting even to talk, share, etc., <u>she</u> doesn't want to. Is this how it goes? I can't <u>bear</u> it! And then, those rare moments of synchronicity, when she wants and I can, and it clicks and we both feel satisfied and enlivened and en-nobled somehow, by the depth of encounter we <u>can</u> have. She is so wise, a <u>wiser</u> child I really have not known. Wisdom is a burden for a child of her age and she's wise enough even to know that. I <u>do</u> wonder what her life will put in front of her and what she'll do with it all.

*

I so enjoy (my daughter) these days — watching her growing in her thinking — always observing and trying to see what's going on between people, what's being said. She starts lots of interesting talks — like <u>why</u> does that man think television should be eliminated? — the book, *Four Arguments for the Elimination of Television* — How can (our friend) smoke seven cigarettes in two hours? — Isn't it amazing Helen Keller could 'experience' Niagara Falls? etc. You can almost see her expanding her consciousness, building her awareness.

*

(Our twelve year old's) birthday was very nice. She was very happy with her gifts, the meal, etc. and said so lovingly. She looks so beautiful in her dress — and in her clown costume. It's hard to believe she can be twelve — though she is so mature and tall and self-possessed. Still the memory of her as a baby is strong in me — always that perky look in the eye — the quickness and ready laugh. She is such a joy for me — a gift of a daughter.

A Circus (party) is just right for this age — they all had wonderful costumes and acts — they loved doing them and kept inventing more. They were so appreciative of the party — (our daughter) too — which made us see again how important it is to do these kinds of things with children — to give them the time and preparation and interest. Eleven/ twelve-year-olds love to act — they are not too self-conscious — they like to dress up/make-up/ be behind a kind of mask/ explore ways of being.

✳

(At 12) Generally she's been lovely this summer, enjoying her friends, her visage in the mirror, new ways of wearing old clothes, new hair styles... and even enjoying her family. She's — as always — <u>fiercely</u> independent but lately very affectionate, sitting herself on my knee at every opportunity. Since she is almost as big as me, that's not always easy...but very nice. She's got on with (her younger sibling) fairly well too. I do enjoy her growing up.

*

I've also taken a new step with (my young teenage daughter) I think. We've had lots of good talks. Outwardly she can be just as frustrating, aggressive, foul mouthed, but inwardly there is something new and positive in our relationship... I've always trusted our relationship and felt it strong and full of love. So it is now, but with some new special quality connected with her growing ability to express herself and her uniqueness. I've learned not to predict one day from another and to be prepared for loving conversation, storms, tears, or just rude dismissal. I've also especially had time to enjoy her humor and brightness and her incredibly mischievous spirit.

*

It was so nice to finally have (a distant friend's daughter) over — the night before her birthday, and we are looking forward to her coming tomorrow night. She looks beautiful of course...although I try to look with (her mother's) eyes and wonder — is she too thin? She was sweet with us and seems happy. We were very impressed with her and how 'grown up' she was. She seems — and that is also, I guess, her big effort — to be even older than she is, with older kids, older conversation. Still she is 15 and that does seem, suddenly pretty grown up. I still remember her when (we) first met, sucking her thumb, taking naps. Those years do seem to have gone quickly. Suddenly we are mothers of teenagers. Why can't we be closer to help and support each other through all of this?

*

I know what you mean about how vulnerable you are to (your teenager) — how she can hurt you. I feel very open like that with both (my children) frequently these days and am also surprised. I think it's the whole separation process, necessary, etc., but that doesn't help me in the moment. But I know it doesn't help them if I get hurt or sad — it only makes them feel guilty and that of course makes them lash out more later. It's so up and down — (my daughter) can share her thoughts and feelings so deeply with me one minute, we can have such laughter at another time, and then suddenly she'll cut me, yell at me or turn something I have said positively against me. But I'm often pretty moody, too, so maybe I'm equally bewildering to her. In fact I really experience adolescence in myself as well.

CHAPTER 3

Relationships

When the earliest of the letters were being written, most of us were in our late twenties, and the letters span the years until our early forties. Relationships — and specifically long-term partnerships — were central to our daily lives. Many of us were married, and we were trying to form marriages that were different from what we had observed growing up. We wanted to build partnerships of equals with a shared participation in parenting and in opportunities for work. As members of our generation we felt the excitement of exploring new possibilities as women, but also at times an absence of encouragement for what we sought. In the letters we aired our questions, hopes and disappointments, our gratitude and our frustration.

In addition to the challenges of a committed marriage, the letters also address other questions and familiar stress points of the times: divorce, unexpected attractions, same sex relationships. Single friends also shared important insights. In our different ways we were all learning about loving, trying to genuinely care for others and also to value ourselves as independent beings.

Another relational theme that occasionally appears in the letters has to do with our evolving connections with our parents or parents-in-law. We were all trying to build confidence in ourselves as adults, and sometimes this involved freeing ourselves from the legacy of parental judgment. At times there were challenges when our parents came to visit, or even moved in with our families for extended stays. Some of us experienced a tension between the needs of our aging parents and the demands of our daily lives with partners and children.

As in previous chapters, there are references to the idea of reincarnation and karma as a contributing factor in the opportunities and challenges of relationships. There are earnest expressions of knowing that relationships need to be worked on, and that we become ourselves through the mysterious openings and closings that others make possible. The writers share deep and complicated questions about the nature of close connections and also speak of their very personal revelations within the efforts of everyday life.

1974 – 1975

I've been thinking about the struggle between the old idea/ reality/tradition of the 'supporting wife' and a new concept of two beings mutually and consciously supporting the development of each other. The former was serving — to subservient, secondary in terms of choices — this was both her desire — ? — and that of her husband. She was often adored and believed to be "what sustains me," etc., but this was through her unending and giving service. Increasingly, women cannot fill this role — do not consider ourselves as secondary...*want* to be part of a really supporting marriage — yet within the woman the past and future are often in conflict. And the man too may want the future idea but find that life has unconsciously led him to expect the traditional wife's role.

What is it to be a woman now? Reincarnation and karma can offer some answers to the individual, but what of the broader society?

I keep thinking of (two friends') separation and see it as a symbol of the times. A strong, talented, warm woman who cannot find her place in this present world — cannot discover what she wants to 'be.' She wants both a family and a real career, yet the involvement she feels she must give to either is inhibited by her desire for the other. So, indecision, unhappiness, a search for exciting fillers — in her case some extension of Peace Corps and free traveling student days. The need to make a decision and be stuck with its ramifications and responsibilities can cause inaction, panic, escape. And there seem to be so many innocent victims — the woman herself, the husband, who in many cases supports her desires as he can understand them and in no traditional way dominates her. Perhaps it is the most sensitive and compromising — about traditional male roles and expectations — of husbands who ultimately are left. Their wives are forced to see that the problem is not so much in the marriage itself but in themselves. But how not to run away?

The same old frustrations and annoyances always crop up. They begin with the mundane — like who can sleep late — but for me always seem to be manifestations of something much deeper. I really feel that (my husband) should/ could be more 'responsible' for the children — in real ways, though I don't mean just in particular events. He lacks foresight and consistency in dealing with them — and basically looks to me to tell him what to do when. It's not that I don't have the same faults, but I resent being left to pick up the pieces after his mistakes. It's enough that I must try to balance out my own errors toward them, but it's too much to have to counteract his too.

My mother arrives tomorrow morning and I wonder so how

it will all go. I know she doesn't *really* want to come live with us — she has always so valued her independence, and now she feels she has no option. But it could work out very well. I must force myself to be conscious of what I say and do, to be open to her, and non-judgmental. There is so much still to understand, and to love.

＊

I realize that what I so much dislike is having so much about my external life in some sense dependent on (my husband) — the good, bad or indifferent. Even if I try to take control, he can so easily wreck it — i.e. last night needing to leave the meeting before it was over — not intentionally, of course. I am sorry for him because he always feels so badly afterwards — but it is always afterwards. This whole thing of his being away is very difficult for me because sometimes I really resent his being back. At least when he is away, I am responsible for my own time and actions. When I am unhappy I just see him as causing me more trivial work, more emotional turmoil and usurping my free time. I don't know how this can all resolve itself — he can't — perhaps shouldn't — change very fast and I don't like the martyr role.

＊

I have been wondering about the 'Being' of a relationship/ marriage: Is it the creation of both — did it exist first? — what brings people together? It watches over — does this diminish over the years? I think it speaks, *acts* in crisis times, but must be nourished — allowed to grow, given space. What does it need? — Shared space — environment, home; Shared outlook — values, philosophy, religious ideas; Shared creations — children, home, garden, milieu, time spent together, i.e. reading, working, planning, etc. Recreation — socializing, fun, warmth, rest; Sense of purpose — goal — for the individuals but also as a *Being*; Spontaneity — life-giving thrusts. It must be *remembered* and be allowed to speak.

What is the development of the Being — stages — crisis points — new needs? How similar is this to individual development? What are the various stages? What is the relation of children to this Being? Or does it grow into some family Being — is that different?

What happens to the Being as a marriage really goes wrong? — in a divorce? Can a Being be carried — cared for — by only one? — for how long? Or is there then no Being there?

Could this be an exercise idea: have a couple create the Being of the relationship — in words, paint, clay — together or separately — then speak about each other's images — find difficult places — what nourishment is needed?

＊

The little you said, rings through me as another manifestation of what I see as one of the greatest problems of our times — i.e. women — or rather what it is to be a woman. For me personally this is a most urgent question and of course in our society there is no end of examples of the struggles surrounding the question. Unfortunately, so much effort is wasted on the politicizing of the issue. But in myself and in many of my friends, I see a terrible tension — to call it 'motherhood versus career' is to make it absurdly superficial. On the one hand one has talents and professional desires and expectations, and on the other a traditional role/pattern <u>and</u> something instinctive that says the old role isn't all wrong. Then one is highly educated, but for what? One wants to be free — but what is that? And how does it relate to 'love'? In me also was the urge to do exciting, meaningful things, yet a real shying away from ultimate responsibility — from choice about my <u>own</u> life. Because when one makes a choice, then other avenues are cut off — life becomes more fixed, more sedate? — more stable. Traditionally women found the stability in their lives through their husbands. Now we do not want to accept this, but we often are unable to find it ourselves — or perhaps we think we do not want it.

Anyway, the tensions make real work or real motherhood incredibly difficult — to say nothing of our marriages, and so all sorts of things get blamed for what ultimately is a most personal problem. I don't mean to suggest that there are not many external things worthy of blame, but not in an absolute sense. It is difficult to find answers even — especially? — if one knows the problem lies within one. In some sense, I feel very lucky that I had (a child) so early, because that forced me into a position of responsibility that I could not shirk, but that I would have had difficulty choosing.

✳

From a recently divorced friend

(While visiting friends) I excused myself and left them to themselves and I had hope of saving sleep. But they put a record on, and I could hear (the woman) laugh and a conversational tone I always associated back as a child hearing voices coming from my parent's bedroom, of two people talking who were finally and at last alone after a long day and could talk to each other unguardedly. Whether they were arguing or happy — it was my image I heard and felt — of intimacy between two friends. A special world that all are not privileged to — talking at night. There is such a world in those three words. The loss of that privilege is sometimes overwhelming to me. And here I was again — a spectator — in someone else's house — someone else's room — someone else's things and music — someone else's creativity of surroundings....

✳

I wonder so what binds us together. God, I wish I could get some real feelings for karma — what we all bring each other — potentially. And actually — where we come from, where we're going.

*

The whole question of my mother is so difficult. How to help her to want to have her own life? We do want our own life — that becomes clearer — but what really is best for her? She said tonight that to stay with us is "the line of least resistance" and that unless we "throw her out" she will probably just stay. She doesn't want to "fight" anymore. And of course she doesn't want to be alone and hurt any more either. But it's not right for her to just give up — she's not that old and she still has so much to give others — and herself. But now we are all stifled — she because she has no life, house, friends, interests of her own, and we because she sits in on ours. She needs people, and we do too — but in very different ways. Pride of ownership/ possessions/ surroundings are important to her, but in another way also very important to me. Perhaps the lack of open conflicts only makes it all more difficult.

*

For me the question of being a woman is further complicated — although also in some sense aided — by my belief in reincarnation and karma. After struggling through several other avenues, I now see that to come to any real understanding of — and perhaps peace with — myself, I must seek out why I am a woman now — i.e. in terms of my own ego development, and in terms of my position in a society with its current problems. I have many related questions: what is family? what is the meaning of marriage? how can two people really — consciously — help and support each other on their individual paths of development?

∗

Did I ever tell you about a dream I had which ended with (my husband) coming into a room where I was, in (my son's) pajamas — him not me! It was a long, complicated dream. As a mother, it is obvious that one must support, and care for, and in some ways sacrifice some parts of oneself for the being of one's children. With a husband, maybe it's a similar thing — only here one is not so concerned with helping a being to incarnate, but with helping a karma, an impulse, a question to incarnate. I don't know for sure if this is right, but I'm considering it. I trust you don't think I have suddenly turned sweet and always supportive and sappy — there's little likelihood of that — no such luck, as (my husband) would say! It's much more a kind of inner shift that seems to be taking place. In the day-to-day, I still see him with all his endearing qualities <u>and</u> all his unconscious, insensitive ways. And I still complain and feel as justified as ever in my complaints. My bitchier side says, "If I'm to make an inner shift toward you, you better be worthy of it!" — even at a day-to-day level. And even my less bitchy side feels there is truth in that — and so does he.

*

To a friend before her wedding

Of course we are both very happy for you (both), and we wish we could be there for your wedding. Sometimes we do feel sadly far away. But we will be thinking of you and we send you many good wishes — why does it sound so corny to write that?? Anyway, even after all these years and enough troubles, we still feel there is something very real and beautiful and potential about marriage — so we wish you many years of knowing and renewing this in all the many ways possible.

*

Is it harder to have friendships with men *after* one is married? — the subtlety of being a 'wife' in the other's eyes, or a slight loss of mystique even when there was no overt sexual interest. Is a 'soul' relationship a threat to one's marriage? Why more so when with a member of the opposite sex? Do we sometimes indulge in sex because we don't know — yet — where else to put the relationship?

*

After the end of her first marriage to her college boyfriend

I don't know if I wrote about the singles life in San Francisco. It is wild to say the least — quite a bit different from "18 and never been kissed." I am fond of saying — "the last time I was single, I was 19 and a virgin!" There are so many 'singles' in S.F. that the problem isn't 'getting' dates, but rather avoiding them for some peace of mind. There is much superficiality, as you would suspect, but if you take it as that, it can be fun — sailing, tennis, fine restaurants, etc. And it never does hurt one's ego to be treated like a queen once in a while. I do a lot on my own — hiking with my dog, playing the piano, just reading by the fire, as I really am finding a rebirth, too, in privacy. I took a vacation last October on my own to Mexico. I was really feeling a bit weird about going all by myself, but I knew I needed it, so I made the plunge. What a revelation! I can't describe how good it was for me — really got in touch with myself — no outside pressures or expectations.

*

It's not going to be that easy. There is so much about my mother's way of looking at the world that I don't agree with. I don't feel as critical as I used to, but that doesn't mean I like (her views) as they relate to me either. And it is most difficult where this relates to (the children). If *I* don't agree with something in and for myself, I don't feel I must always say so, but when Mother is very analytical with (my daughter) or goes into gory details of illnesses or accidents, etc, then I feel I must at least tell her that I prefer that she not. But I don't want to stifle her being with the children either. There is such a tension between my protectiveness and sense of what is appropriate for the children and my desire not to be critical of her. I must be able to find the balance — I don't want her to feel unwanted, which she isn't, or that I disapprove, which I don't, as regards her own personal being.

＊

Why do we all project? What is the positive role of this in the development of consciousness? — i.e. to open doors that one can go through — or not — to greater self-awareness/ wholeness. Does this wholeness — sense of independence — separate one from the other — make the other unnecessary? I think not — it is a step toward freedom — one can then meet not out of *need* but out of joy — can more really enjoy the masculine and feminine other. The other can — must? — help in finding what belongs to me. But somewhere there is the area beyond help by another — the 'loneliness' one feels as a human being — that one does stand alone in the spiritual world. In a close/love relationship one can more freely experience this loneliness — and allow the other to too. Both know this must be and that they *share* it — and are meant to help each other — to here and beyond.

＊

I know (my husband) needs to be supported, actively loved and yet somehow my abilities to do this get shaky as I ponder the relationship and my struggles with it. I feel I need to also be 'cared for' in some basic inner sense — to be seen and *actively* involved with. I feel we must together develop many things and work to understand who we are and what we bring to each other. He agrees — head — with this in some general way but living from feelings is much harder. He said at some unconscious, culturally produced place, a part of him feels a woman should just take care of the relationship and not make trouble — i.e. leave the man to his 'real' work. Of course, he cannot justify this position — nor does he try to — from any perspective of development, etc., and yet it works on in his actions. And so I feel so frustrated, and left alone — in an inner sense more than outer, which bothered me several years ago. Then I cannot be warm — I put up walls of protection and whole defenses begin to work which say "typical", "can't expect much of him" and all the bitter responses which I don't *want* to feel nor in some inner truth sphere even believe at all. Yet, I don't trust as much as I used to — my faith in him really caring can be very shaky at times.

*

The decision to live with someone again, or make any sort of commitment, is so remote to me now. I hope that will change. One big problem about commitment at this point is the shutting off of other alternatives. There seem to be so many things and people to experience that I find myself in a frenetic state of sampling everything — or wanting to. And the more I see, the more I realize there is to experience — Pandora's Box. But I guess it's just one of those in-between exploratory stages. The lack of direction is a bit unsettling, but "que sera, sera."

It's a big, and probably slow, transition to learn to direct my life on my terms, rather than in reaction to external forces — to think of myself as a unit unto myself, rather than in the context of a male-female relationship. There's a lot of <u>un</u>learning as well as learning to be done. Sometimes I think I'll never make it.

✳

My mother still lives with us—perhaps it will be permanent — although I keep avoiding believing that. Which tells you something about how it is. It's not that it's so bad, but it does have several drawbacks. She is sweet with the children, and she tries hard not to be in the way — it's just that she is always here! And she has her own definite — if superficial — opinions on everything and we seem to waste so much time disagreeing. Not arguing, just not sharing a lot of basic things. She seems to have lost any will to have her own life, which is, of course, as bad for her as it is hard on us. Still, she gets around quite a bit on her own… and perhaps she is building up strength to take her life in her own hands again. I must say, I no longer theorize about the problems of older people — I am much more acutely aware of the very real problems so many people face.

*

(My mother-in-law), my personal Albatross, sojourned almost two weeks... We had a major crisis at week one after which I decided I <u>had</u> to pull myself together, as it was obvious she never would, a conclusion I have reached at least 10,000 times before. I did though, and taught her how to make dolls and showed her card weaving to teach the other grandchildren, etc. Very successful — gave her something to do, which kept her off the housework bit — there was none to do and she couldn't bear it. She couldn't come right out and say your flat is filthy, let me clean it, so she had to sit amongst it — do nothing except <u>allude</u> to cobwebs, etc. You can imagine me at my most maliciously obtuse, on a bad day. We allowed her to do the washing, and she allowed that to become her total pre-occupation, exhausting us all by tearing up and down every 15 minutes to see how it was drying. When the sun finally got it together, and she could take it in, she'd say, "Well, there's a load off our minds, isn't it?" and every time, I would hear myself — even though I vowed each time I <u>would not</u> — say "I couldn't care less" or "I hadn't given that a thought" or whatever. A fairly childish way of asserting myself, wouldn't you say?

· · ·

Did I tell you about the time we were staying with her and she asked us what we wanted for lunch. We said we'd go out and buy some stuff and cook something. Off we went, and when we came back with the ingredients to make curry, she had already <u>cooked</u> a meal… Will we <u>ever</u> be M-in-Laws? Please tell me?!! I <u>already</u> hear the doom bells even in the question, even as I am <u>determined</u> not to be, <u>ever</u>, etc., ad nauseum. Just as I was determined <u>never</u> to be a partner to an 'archetypal M-in-Law/D-in-Law' situation. You know, I just hope that we'll be wise enough by then to make our intellectual realizations into realities. After all, <u>some</u> people do succeed at it.

*

The difficulty of conversations between men and women is a level problem. A man repeats what he thinks a woman meant, and feels he is saying something new. But the woman is disappointed at levels not addressed by the one picked up. Women speak from a soul-experiential sphere; men more in the intellectual realm. Women together support each other in conversation — flow. Men together engage in more sparring.

*

About the problem of friends of the opposite sex — what to talk about with a man? There are so many habitual sexual undertones — seemingly out of place — what is there to share? Why the fear? How to have genuine, caring interest in the other? Are we searching for brothers — in the widest sense?

*

Would a secure, real sense of accomplishment in 'meeting' in a relationship — with active consciousness over *years*, contribute to a better working in the world? And does it — unconsciously? — hinder not to have this?

＊

As for Christmas, it really was very nice — which rather surprised me, since I didn't have enough time to worry about (my parents-in-law) coming, I just didn't and so was myself and really enjoyed seeing them. It was the <u>first</u> time that I really felt they tried to see and hear us — on our terms — and that they had some respect for what they saw and heard. Perhaps this was partial projection of a very baby self-respect/confidence that I feel growing in myself — and no doubt they picked up a lot of my own bad vibes before. But anyway, it was good — and I enjoyed listening to and seeing them, and I tried to enter into conversations on 'their terms' too.

＊

1976

We've been... job hunting with at least one possible opening. If we move, we'll probably convert to 'full-time marriage,' by which I mean home ownership and all the disastrous consequences — like insurance, maintenance, heating bills.

Right now, we have all the fun and none of the responsibilities, but I don't suppose it will continue forever!

*

On the question of trust — how is this built? What is it? What we (in working with spiritual science) can offer is the concept of two people on an evolving path, needing each other for development — trust that the other is developing and has — had — the intention to help me in my development — and vice versa. There is an underlying assumption that people do believe they belong together — that they *want* to work it out.

On the question of one partner 'waiting' for another — i.e. to develop together — can one ask another to wait? How can one want to slow down a bit — for a while — to put the relationship on some more solid ground? How can this more solid ground be achieved? What kind of encouragements, prods? There is a need to spend time together doing/sharing something — i.e. reading together — not so much for what is read but for the act of doing it. Where are the areas where one, alone, must be free? Where can one expect the other to hold back a bit?

*

Perhaps I have never felt so alone. I can hardly touch the many worries within me for lack of anyone to bear them with me — or at least to hear me find myself in some dialogue. I just still cannot really think things 'through' alone — I need someone who really cares and can be by me out of a giving love, not because I beg for it. When I must ask, I become unable to really talk about what most concerns me. Perhaps no one can really help another in that place — but at least they can wait by the door to wish you well as you go in, and be there to greet you on your return.

*

The group spoke about constructive argument — having it rather than it having you. Being able to share a twinkle even if you "aren't finished" being angry. Not being intimidated but not letting destruction reign either.

*

In our women's group, we identified the following questions to do with relationships:
- What insecurity in oneself allows a feeling of intimidation?
- What to do with a situation that intimidates you?
- Why do we seek relationships?
- Why do we choose a 'marriage' relationship?
- What is the *Self* that goes into a relationship?
- How can one make a relationship with oneself? — outside a relationship with another.
- How to avoid the dependency in relationships?
- How much do we seek ourselves in a relationship — and not really the other?

- What is a relationship with someone you don't like?
- How to avoid relationships? Why?
- What kind of consciousness hurts relationships?
- Sex — what is it? Why does it change relationships?
- Phases of a long-term relationship?

∗

Here a friend relates how a couple with whom she had been close the year before, came to visit and surprisingly deep and important conversations took place.

You know, (the man) and I were really close at (college). We talked probably on the average of two hours a day. Sometimes we skipped classes just to talk and we talked a lot about men and women and various types of relationships, our pasts, mind-blowing situations we were or expected to be in, etc. It was pretty intimate, but I must say completely honestly that neither of us flirted with the other — ever — and that one killer issue never came up. All of which was coupled with my belief that they had this amazing relationship, and it was new, and I was not interested in screwing it up. At one point, in fact, (the woman) came up to us really bummed out and he went off with her and I said to myself — that's it — having realized that there was something he wasn't telling me, I decided to back out. A week later, of course, he insisted on knowing why I was being so aloof, but we didn't get back to the same depth as before. — sorry for all the detail about a past situation.

When they came this time, (she) and I sat and I was telling her about (the college) this year and she told me why she was so unhappy there. Then she started talking about how jealous she was of me then. It was so interesting because she knew just what it was like to be 'single' and on close terms with a married man so she didn't hate me or mistrust me. She just spent the whole year crying. The point was that she couldn't understand why he wouldn't share my friendship with her. Meanwhile, he was sort of testing his perceptions of women through me, as well as his ability to lead his own life while married and committed to her. I just can't tell you what a relief it was for both (the woman) and me to be talking this out. A day and a half later the three of us got into it. It was incredible. I mean, this is all a year and a half later and here none of us really expected to see one another again, let alone expose such tender stuff and believe me, all three of us exposed a lot of vulnerability. As it ended, we all got through it and it felt like we were freed to carry on with these relationships in a newer, more honest way. Phew — it was heavy — but the vibes were so positive and love-filled.

You know how I feel about confrontations like this. You just have to allow yourself to be stretched and take what that brings — pain, joy, the works. The thing I wonder about is if I've got it figured out yet, if I can deal with these relationships in a healthy way yet or if another weird one is going to come my way that will throw all my well-formed theories. Like, I feel now that never again will I let the #1 woman be excluded. Shit, I wish you were here and it's the same old theme with yet another variation and I want to talk to you, damn it.

*

I find myself in a situation which is almost too obvious to describe in an objective way. First, let me remind you that I am 35. Now let me try to set the scene — there is a person also 35, apprentice at a local school, married before, without children....

Now — I must also say that he is attractive, but that's beside the point! For some reason, we are attracted to each other, and we are both trying to see this in a responsible, conscious way, as well as being quite aware of the tremendous force that this relationship seems to be living in. Our relationship consists of conversations which are of a most special kind. There is an essence in them which really seems to reach my inner-most being.

It is very difficult to live with... but, I trust that coming through it all, will result in a better understanding of my relationship with (my husband). I consider the fact that he and I have just finished our first seven years together, that meeting my friend — and that is really what I consider him to be — at this time in my life seems most remarkable. But and here is the big question that I am facing — is he just a 'distraction' which would in fact hinder whatever I am destined to do with (my husband)?! I remember Helen Salter saying "Destiny is when you meet 'another' man; Karma is what you do about it!"

I know my relationship with (my friend) will stay on a very 'spiritual level' — but that to me is why it is such an enormous problem and question — because after all, that is where I want my relationship with (my husband) to be. It also seems to be very alive in a soul sense.

The moment I sensed all this beginning, I asked (my husband) for a day alone — I tried to find again where in fact he was and is. I suppose I wanted <u>not</u> to notice the reality that I was missing something. I told him that I was needing and or enjoying the attention from a certain individual too much. I wasn't specific, but I think the message came through on a subconscious level.

So my dear friend — now what do I do?!... It seems quite clear to me that I would not hurt (my husband) or my children — so that leaves me in a pretty obvious place — right here!

＊

I am writing to you today because I feel I would like to touch on an area with you that is of vital importance to me — I say "touch on" because I have a feeling that I will have difficulty verbalizing my thoughts & feelings on the matter. It has of course, to do with my relationship — not specifically but as a total question. I have decided that because of my very significant relationship with (my husband), that any other relationship must of course take on a limited form — that form however has the potential of being of the highest and most limitless nature — it has the potential of bringing the highest self out in each — though all the obvious temptations are very much part of it all, it is an incredible opportunity to overcome and strengthen the egos which are confronting one another.

My question lies in the area of individual growth vs. loyalty, commitment, love, guilt arising out of conditioning, energy, truthfulness, etc, etc, etc... I know that it will be almost impossible for (my husband) to understand it on a non-threatening level, let alone accept it. So I must risk it & either be totally open & honest, which is my impulse, or to "spare" (my husband) the potential hurt, thereby perhaps depriving him of growth, self-questioning & our growth together as life partners.

✳

The question of needs comes up again and again — always in relation to one's own — i.e. not to what we may or may not bring to others. "One person can't meet all *my* needs" — but we (don't) talk much of the other side — how free we can leave another.

✳

(A woman friend), while living with (a man), has a woman lover as well, a really beautiful woman with whom she spends weekends and goes away with. We got into talking about sexuality and personhood in ways different from what I'm used to. If you were in the States, you'd see what a big thing gayness is. As some indication, all the situation comedies on TV that everybody, including kids, watches have gay people and gay issues on regularly. With (my friend), I wasn't surprised; in fact, I knew about it intuitively. It just seems like one other facet of herself she has to explore and be conscious of and it in no way bothers me. She is so into women! We always talked about how many good, strong, seeking women we knew, and how few good men we knew. It seems to me that a physical relationship with a woman is a natural continuation — culmination? — of that attitude — especially among women who are able to cultivate such strong, binding relationships, anyway. I am so involved with (my boyfriend) right now that I have no interest in complicating us with any other really intimate relationship, but I don't know where that's coming from. I don't know why I'd say I'd never have a sexual relationship with a woman, except that the idea doesn't appeal to me — like married men — and that it's always such a mess. But like my (ethnic background), I've always accepted my heterosexuality. It's comfortable like that, but I never considered that I really had a choice. My choice is to leave myself like that, but it gnaws on me when so many people I know are loving both men and women — Why not?? Does this ever come up in your women's group discussions? In the US, no women's group could bypass it — especially among women who trust each other and really speak together intimately. I'm so curious to know what you think. I mean, we all think women are so neat, so why don't we get more intimately involved with each other? I think it's easier for a woman who hasn't been physically involved with many men or types of men and relationships to say — why bother, who needs the complications, etc, etc, but for those of us who get in messy situations and then appreciate the 'experience' — good or bad — it's another possibility to be reckoned with.

✳

The realm between sex and no sex is vast — the realm of the sensual — of contact, touching, warmth sharing. Do we fear this with other women because of some lurking fear that one thing would lead farther than we were prepared to go?... Also there is the question why *should* a relationship go into the physical? What are the cultural pressures working both ways?

✳

(We spoke about the) question of one's love for women friends being a threat to our husbands — i.e. someone spoke of them almost as lovers, and he felt upset. I asked (my husband) about this later and he said he had felt it — felt a kind of jealousy when I spoke, for example about my love for (my woman friend). We had a good talk about this — about the nature of different loves and how the more you love, the more you can love. I do feel this — though perhaps there are boundaries. My love for (my woman friend) is one of a clear recognition of an *old* relationship — the *joy* of seeing her again. With (my husband) it is completely different — we must *live* together — grow ever more to know each other. With other friends there are again other qualities. I am only beginning to appreciate all this — to see my many sides, their needs and gifts.

*

1977 – 1980

I've been thinking about the idea that everyone needs more than one person to satisfy different parts of themselves. Security in (one primary) relationship allows for other friendships — recognizes the need for them.

*

The question of why *one* exclusive relationship made me suddenly have a new thought — it is something of our western culture — not in all societies — but why is this? Could this be a cultural/evolutionary need related to the *need* of masculine and feminine coming together in a new way? — i.e. in an ongoing developing, struggling, *conscious* relationship we can learn about — and bring into culture — a real relationship of masculine and feminine — a real and positive balance. Marriage *can* be a means to this — though of course many forces struggle to keep this from happening... empty marriage, divorce, degradation of sex, etc. The question calls for some understanding of the positive — and negative — of *real* feminine and masculine possibilities in each — quite beyond roles. Only two real individuals can have a real relationship. They may develop their individuality through the relationship but they must be whole, secure in themselves — to some extent.

When you told us in our group that it was such a relief for you to realize that you really loved other people outside of your marriage, I was so glad to hear that. There are a number of people in my life for whom I have the same feelings of love, but I never admitted it to myself. I'm so glad you helped me to discover that.

I don't know where to begin, but I will try. So much has happened... After writing to you last time it became clear that I was in fact experiencing something which felt very much like finding a different me again, the me that I just hadn't known for a while. It became equally clear that it was most important to be in touch with what that was, and make some very conscious decisions as to how and where to go from that point. One thing was quite clear, in no way could I consider a relationship that would take my energy from (my husband) and our children.

Now as I write, I must say that even though I came to my independent decisions, my friend and I were in total agreement of that priority. The only way we could even consider being special friends was if it would not involve a sexual relationship. We even made some basic rules, which may sound a little funny but they were necessary. So we embarked on a relationship which everyone in my life including me had always said would be impossible. They just don't exist — I thought — but, if as I have learned, there is a deeper and more disciplined caring which has to come from both concerned, it is not only possible, but those forces can be transformed into something quite beautiful and strength-giving which carries you to the next stage of the relationship — which lives more in the realm of the soul. The beauty was and is in the real caring about each other as human beings — which so often gets lost in my marriage — and maybe many other marriages.

As we looked at our relationship, consciousness seemed to be the word that came up frequently. He being very conscious on all the levels that seem to be important, having to do with recognizing and tuning in on the highest and deepest aspects of soul and spirit meetings. Living through day after day in recognition that the potential in human relationships was quite beyond my highest expectations gave me the absolute trust, and it seemed that it was quite right, to share my new friendship with (my husband). In other words (my friend) has become not only my good friend, but also a friend to (my husband).

I must go back a moment, (my husband) does not know of the 'work' we had to do to evolve to that point, that was really something that belonged to me alone. If I had had a sexual relationship, then I would not have felt that it was mine alone and would have wanted to share that in a different way with (my husband).

(My friend) has played a very important part in our marriage... Let me go back again, however — my relationship with (my friend) lives in the 'recognition' of our experience. We have made what we felt an important discovery which came out of each action which we felt was totally truthful and conscious. That discovery has to do with the fact that male-female relationships have the potential of unfolding in a most unique way — though it's true that relationships start at different points, i.e. sexual attraction, intellectual attraction, spiritual, etc — one can — or I should say, two can — quite consciously be in touch with the stages of unfoldment. There is a paradox because while it seems important that one can't direct the course on the one hand, one's consciousness and free choice — 'free' meaning being aware of the so called laws and consequences — play a very important part in the unfoldment....

(My friend) and I meet here at our house every Tuesday night. We started a study... (My husband) is very supportive of our studies, and I am finding it very interesting to say the least.

*

We are having a good holiday time. It takes always more than a week to meet each other *(she and her husband)* again as friends. First, we have to forget and forgive a lot of the pervious months, many antagonistic feelings, etc, etc. It is difficult to really know in what way we can make a new start, a different start so we can take up what we've learned from last year.

*

How on earth can we ever make clear to men, to our own husbands, that they have responsibility for family life and marriage? They only feel threatened and they know how to talk to us as if it is not such a problem. They close themselves to this truth and they throw it back to us as if we are the ones who always have problems — 'Oh, you have your period?'

I <u>know</u> it is impossible to press your partner to give, to offer love because it won't work. But I can't stop asking for it. I can't stop trying to make it <u>clear</u>, so he will understand. But he only feels that I force him to be different than he wants to be, and he closes himself off stronger than before.

*

It was so good what you wrote this summer: "I decided to <u>love</u> our fights and crises. I experience how we do grow because of them"... When I want to love our crises, I must be able to open myself. It is the capacity of creating light. Slowly, slowly I get the courage to do it. It would help me much if you could describe the process in your coming out of a fight and to direct yourself again to positivity. How do you feel in such a turning process?

*

I sure wish we could both grow sufficiently to stop the non-sense and get on with all the work outside that is calling to be answered. I can't even write about it all and I wish it were all gone so that I could look forward... without all these pressures of where I should be with my children. I don't even know at this moment what the best thing is for the children. Am I supposed to be the enlightened, recep-tive, forgiving and loving female — just holding back so that someday I will grow sufficiently — if and when I have been able to do all the above and more — and that then (my husband) or anyone else will also grow by the Saint-like examples I will have set?!! I think that is what I am <u>supposed</u> to do! But shh! I don't feel like it at the moment!!!

*

I don't like that I play 'judgment' to (my husband's) expansiveness. Why do I do it?/feel I have to do it? It's a basic dynamic in our relationship — sometimes good, sometimes a pain.

*

I find it hard with my Mom here. And it makes me feel so guilty that I can't just enter in and really enjoy conversations. She is sweet and helpful and means so well. Partially it's that I feel so strung out anyway — so many things weighing on my consciousness.

*

Yesterday was our 13th anniversary... I feel like we have always been married — my whole adulthood has unfolded within this relationship. We seem on a kind of plateau now — a secure, supportive, pleasant one but without much intensity. We are both too busy — and together we so easily tend to look forward. We need to stop a bit and look around and live into where we are now.

*

1981 – 1985

After a recent divorce

The move has not been easy — the practical side you know only too well... I wish I could make a clean break with the past, but it will still take a while. Inwardly, it has been very hard at times — a feeling of destruction of the past — maybe also a deeper knowledge that the past must find another positive form for the future — so many unfinished threads in relationship with (my ex-husband). I must come to terms with what we <u>did</u> build up, and the house, or certain parts of it, were expressions of this... Slowly I begin to feel better in myself. I think the decision for divorce was the last step in a long process — not as it is for some where it is often the first, or in the middle. I feel now it must be a process of building up — both in myself but also in relation to (him). I guess I must expect some difficulties but I feel fairly optimistic.

*

During the Ariadne workday in our talks about family life — revolving mainly around working consciously with and loving those who come into our family who are not 'relations' — step-children, boarders, etc — and also with blood ties — how to bring consciousness in this area as blood ties on their own are no longer enough — I realized that in whatever we do on family life, we must bring in the element of karma to really begin to understand our relationships... What is it we especially learn and develop through being connected by blood? What do those relationships offer and what do they exclude or limit? I know it's a simple thought, but somehow it struck me anew how an understanding of karma and reincarnation lifts the question of relationships onto a different level — frees it. We seemed to talk a lot about blood ties, examples of irrelevance — of when it seemed to hold no special bond — and ones where they have been important; of where we have felt closer to non-relations than relations; about what to do with blood relationships, what their meaning is, how because we expect them to work we don't immediately bring as much consciousness to them as to step-children, boarders, etc. so we run into trouble often. Also the importance for children of family ties... We talked about the positive side of feeling a certain detachment from our children — not to possess. And on and on.

*

Her husband was away for a year of study.

This year has been one of living 'in between.' No past — that means not the possibilities I had last year, no future yet. Just 'here and now.' It has been really a very good year. I feel very happy with it. My living alone was very welcome — although alone is just alone, and to do everything alone is a lot! But I felt space to digest our past. (My husband) and I have had a very good and intensive correspondence. It is really fruitful to write things, to put questions and to have a week or more to let this 'come down' in the other person so he can answer in a more secondary way.

Being alone, creating my own <u>culture</u>, in the house and with the children as well as in myself has been very important. The experience of 'being alone is good and fruitful' and 'being together is good and fruitful' — just both in a more equal way. I hope very much that we'll be able to make space for both of these elements in the future. I mean actually <u>I</u> hope that <u>I'll</u> be able to <u>continue</u> my own 'being alone' culture beside what I want and will share in daily life with (my husband).

❋

Although I can laugh and wonder about almost being a freak if one is married for any length of time today, I know in my heart to build and create a nourishing love between two people is probably the most important work to do for the world, but one of the hardest.

❋

(My husband's) parents came on Friday and left this afternoon. I really enjoyed them and so enjoyed cooking them nice meals, etc. (My husband's) father seemed more relaxed than he ever has been in our house, and well, it was just such a good visit for all of us.

❋

A growing relationship demands continuously the willingness to become disturbed in your own 'harmony' by your partner. The willingness to open-up your own order — balance — attitude and receive the influence of your partner, to undergo the 'chaos' and to have the faith that a new order — balance will be found again, which also will be true to yourself and true to your partner. It is a wonderful process, but I need to develop much courage and power and faith to enter in these confrontations!

You showed in what you wrote, your willingness to look in <u>yourself</u> for the reason a fight comes up. Recently I read in Steiner: "As long as we feel the need to blame anyone or anything else for what happens with us, we are incapable of making a <u>serious step</u> on the path of (inner development)." It is true, for sure! It is really fruitful if we can practice this knowledge in our relationship with our partners.

You wrote also that by having a hard summer you peeled off a level and so came closer to each other. In this I can agree very much, painful processes do make us more humble and make us realize that mutual incapacity is a reality with which we have to live.

*

The one problem is that all summer we have not been together as a family without work commitments of one kind or another. So now we have a week and a thousand things that need attention or they will remain undone all year and so naturally the first few days home we have had the quarrel that's been put off all summer — old theme with new variations and anxieties and expectation. The kids weren't even especially spared and somehow this evening we were all sitting at the table with teary eyes wondering how to move the situation. (Our oldest child) was analyzing both of our faults with accuracy yet impudence, but something moved, and we can begin to work... but on what — acceptance, or change, or both and how?... There are certain aspects of our relationship which are flourishing but other areas that are cramped, suffering and unattended. And can we hold a vision of a wholeness and work towards it? Will we, can we, create something out of nothing — because I think the marriage we are striving for is new, without patterns, hardly born, just emerging? We don't know what we want — when we try to tell each other, we easily get caught in old expectations or false imaginations. I wish I could talk to you.

Things have been fairly quiet since we came back. My mother is feeling happy, and I try to think of little things to please her, like taking her to the forest where the heather is a sea of purple bloom. She has been very housebound and will be so again this winter, so the shortest trip is an event for her.

✳

After a death in the community

The reality of how quickly death can come — any time — made our quarrel seem so petty and absurd. We can never wait and say, when the children grow up, or tomorrow, or in a year, we will have more time or things will be different. We can only love now, each moment. We don't know about tomorrow, yet we continually fail to see what, when faced with death, is only what endures and is real.

✳

My mood has deteriorated, via 'circumstances' to something like black upon red upon black. Resentment/anger/resentment. The final straw has just broken my back, and I would like to scream, or piss off, or cry for about two hours. None of which would help, so I won't do any of them, I guess. It's all so trivial, and men are such utter <u>SHITS</u>. And the worst thing of all, is that by tomorrow, I'll have decided none of it is worth haggling about and nothing will change.

✳

When (my husband and children) went away those two days, especially after Christmas, I felt devastated for a while. As though I had to see things in perspective — what endless time — without children's illnesses, fights, problems, demands, without housework, without an ongoing relationship with an adult, without quarrels and expectations and disappointments — would be like. Nothing would have much meaning. How lonely single working women — or men — must be, unless they have real relationships — not just affairs and acquaintances.

*

My parents' stay went fine and I am very glad they came although I was rather exhausted and relieved when they went. I felt we never quite relaxed together, that they weren't really comfortable in England, with the heat they didn't count on and with our apparently strange ways, although I tried to be my most normal. Our conversations never went very deep — maybe if we saw each other more often they could though there was potential; important things were brought up but then left without really being developed. I think they would have opened up more 'on their own ground,' in their own surroundings. Anthroposophy, although not spoken about much, seemed a kind of threat. But they met enough of our friends and (the children's) friends, if only briefly, to also realize something of the positive qualities of our life here, the school and college, the supportive caring environment. They of course probably loved most of all getting to know the children again, especially at such a blossoming time for both of them. In spite of their worries about academic and material achievement for them — and our lack of materialism — they couldn't fail to recognize their physical and inner health, and brightness, their active imaginations and strength of character…. They seemed to tire very easily. They are getting old.

*

Things have been awful between (my husband) and me when we've had any real time together, which isn't often, so mostly the surface looks quite smooth. But underneath levels are disintegrating. The physical bond suffers through lack of time and because the soul bond has the same old unresolved complications. So when there is 'time' we use it to explore all the old defenses, rejections, expectations, regrets, etc. Spiritually, our bond is strong and clear and wonderful… we are friends and we do have things to share… Well that's putting it pretty schematically but of course all the levels interweave and I have been miserable mainly because a few times I have come close to actually 'seeing' our doubles[1]

---

1   The reference in the above excerpt to the 'double' is another idea that comes from Rudolf Steiner's picture of the human being. This is similar to what Jung speaks of as the 'shadow'. Briefly, the double refers to those aspects of our self that remain in an untransformed state — our unconscious habits and unattended ways of being that have been building up throughout our life. As we approach middle age, some of this begins to rise to consciousness and ask for our attention, yet we can often resist the self-knowledge being offered and insist to ourselves and others that "I'm not really like that." In long-term partnerships we can sometimes focus on

fighting each other, but feeling helpless as to what to do. It doesn't help that we have our conversations on into the early hours of the morning. All sorts of hallucinations and misunderstanding are possible. Also, the same old themes recur and I wonder, don't we <u>ever</u> grow?... I feel like many aspects of our difficulties seem like a kind of adolescence — we'll be entering our 15th year soon.

I have been through terrible turmoil in the last two months, being depressed and wanting to change things in our relationship (with my husband), being critical and saying the wrong things. How often have I thought of you and longed to have a good long talk. When will I come to terms with a less than perfect relationship and try to improve it in the <u>right</u> way? I try to keep the balance between criticism and acceptance, but it is a narrow line. In this respect I experience the masculine within me and the feminine in him. But does criticism have to be cold? I don't think so.

---

what is really the double of the other, with all its irritating qualities, as a way of avoiding our own need to work on ourselves. In repetitive arguments, it is often the doubles of the couple who are behind the reoccurring patterns. For there to be any real change, the individuals must choose to bring consciousness to the moment and try something new.

*

I too struggle with dullness. I feel I'm not really moving — not very interested or interesting — or inspired. Again, this feeling of lack of direction, lack of will. I always seem to be busy. I love my work and mostly I enjoy (the family), but part of me is very tired and in need of new inspirations and directions. I even, in a fanciful way, began to wonder if I needed a lover! (My husband) and I had a stupid discussion all about this one night; I'm not sure I'd know how to attract a lover if I wanted one. Ah well, maybe it's not the answer anyway.

*

Nice to be by the sea. Nice to be in a tent. Nice to be away from <u>it all</u>, even though I like <u>it all</u>, in itself — nice to be with the kids without any of the other pulls away, especially for a week. Both of us are quite good at relaxing — we both have a very quick wind-down time, find it easy to switch gears, both up and down. We are camping in a natural basin, formed by sand dunes, with scrubby trees growing out of the sides, over the sand dunes is the sea... The kids play in the sand, play in the tent and play in the water. I contemplate the full catastrophe and revel in the fact that I spend almost no time at all doing housework, which continues to be <u>the</u> thing I hate most, having not yet mastered the art of Zen sweeping, washing up, washing clothes, etc, etc, etc.

＊

How hard I find it to have a real relationship with (my husband) at the moment. Too much seems dead, routine. We are fantastic (with shared commitments), but that consumes much of our life. Family life, married life all seems in a rut, uncreative, unloving... I talk about developing a true interest in the other, but I don't think <u>we</u> manage here. Anyway, I long to talk to you about all this — there really isn't anyone else to talk with at this level.

＊

I have heard that (mutual friends) have separated — is that true? More and more I just feel sad when people I know break up. I want us all to make it — together I guess — and I know more all the time of the <u>real</u> difficulties.

＊

I think we will be ok now — if we can keep courage to face the nothingness and honesty to face each other and don't let time and outer activities swirl us away until we don't know each other.

CHAPTER 4

Outer and Inner Development

So often in the letters there are meanderings and questions about the ways we were or were not developing as individuals, wives, mothers, friends, or even daughters, and also in our inner possibilities. There are revelations of self-doubts, judgments about our own laziness, and recognitions of qualities needing to be worked on — such as patience, trust, clearer thinking, or more rhythm in daily life. Sometimes these comments refer to the temperaments, with reference to the fourfold picture of basic personality types elaborated by Rudolf Steiner: Melancholic, Phlegmatic, Sanguine, and Choleric. There is also an awareness of certain landmarks in a biographical timeline that seem to be particularly significant. Many of us had studied Rudolf Steiner's ideas about seven-year life phases — in terms of both child and adult development

— and our own lives offered us ongoing research material, especially for the years between 28 and 42.[1]

Like so many people in the 1970's, many of the writers were on, or at least considering taking up, a path of inner schooling. And this was coupled with a clear sense of the relationship between outer behavior and inner work. One resounding question comes again and again in a variety of forms: "How can I live what I believe?" There are acknowledgements that invitations to development come toward us not only in the challenges of evolving self-knowledge, but also through the very real needs that others present, and also in the ways that others mirror parts of ourselves back to us — including aspects we may not yet have consciously noticed. The idea that we actually find ourselves through others underlies much of what is written here.

The sometimes frustrating realization that develop-ment is a slow process appears frequently. As the writers

---

1   For a more extensive treatment of the four temperaments or the seven-year life phases, see my book *Why on Earth? — Biography and the Practice of Human Becoming*, (Steiner Books, 2013), so much of which was stimulated by my work over the years with many of the friends quoted in this present book. Many other books also address these topics, including: *Taking Charge: Your Life Patterns and Their Meaning* by Gudrun Burkhard (Floris); *Phases* by Bernard Lievegoed (Hawthorn); and the *Biography and Life Cycles* workbooks by Lee Sturgeon-Day.

are growing older, there is an increasing intensity in the recognitions that both outer change and inner growth take time and require regular attention and practice. Committing thoughts, doubts and intentions to paper and sharing self-realizations, questions, and efforts with another were ways of taking small steps forward.

1973 – 1975

I am beginning to see how easy it is to project one's own insecurities outward and thus see in the actions of others toward you things which foster those insecurities. I'm sure that a lot of my difficulties of feeling that no one takes 'me' seriously as an individual apart from (my husband) are encouraged by my own self-doubts. People pick up these doubts in me and so don't pay much attention or expect much from me. <u>Some</u> people are also just plain unfair, but I am beginning to feel that it's as much my own fault as theirs. Is this making any sense? Anyway, I feel that I must come more into an understanding of myself before I can really expect anyone else to. If I can see clearly and honestly my own strengths and weaknesses, perhaps I can meet the world more openly and with more realistic expectations.

✳

I guess even archetypal sanguines can have melancholic moments! — and in fact 1973 tried hard to push me over onto the melancholic side of the scale. Actually, I feel as if I am just beginning to come to some understanding of my 'self' — of who I am after the many sheaths of life begin to fall away. I feel myself becoming gradually less caught up in all the externals of my life and am trying to see what lies behind my actions and my feelings. I don't like a lot of things that I must realize about myself, but still I feel quite hopeful that some positive growth could come out of my turning more inward than I am naturally inclined to do.

From the perspective of the phases of human development the above statement is quite characteristic of a 28-year-old, which was the age of this writer.

*

Do you know that I am almost completely unable to think? By that I mean pursue some thought alone in my head. I find that I spill over with ideas — of mixed quality — when I am in a stimulating conversation, or if I make myself write I can develop thoughts, or if I listen to others talk I have exciting ideas flit through my head. But on my <u>own</u>, it's incredibly difficult for me to stay with any thought — in true sanguine fashion, I jump from one thing to another and constantly allow myself to be bombarded by sense

impressions. So I must try to learn to discipline myself —
internally and externally — but it is so hard!

✳

Why is it tonight when I really feel I have accomplished something — reading and thinking — I *haven't* done the dishes
and the house isn't really picked up?? The story of my life....

✳

About the note from your mother — I can certainly see why
you feel as you do about it, but I keep thinking that whatever she did think or feel, she never <u>consciously</u> felt that way.
I can't read into her subconscious of 20 years ago — and
she has always viewed the world — not just you — in that
sarcastic, I don't-need-or-want-anyone way. Perhaps you can
really use the note now in a positive way — in terms of your
own self-understanding and growth — it sounds from what
you said that you are doing this. I always have trouble doing
anything about my 'self-discoveries.' I have the tendency to
say "ah, yes, that's how I was/am" and even though I hate it, I
change only very slowly, if at all. But still, a clear understanding is a beginning — if only the clear understandings weren't
so painful when they occur!

✳

It's clear that I choose not to write or I would find a way
to make the time. And so I slide on and days go by and I

do not force myself to make anything clear in myself or to see how time and I evolve. Nor do I write down the things about the children which are worth recording — if only because in writing them down I put them consciously into my own being. Of course, that's the real problem — I resist the *effort* necessary for consciousness. I know that the act of writing is for me a positive exercise — a way of practicing so that someday perhaps I can 'think' in solitude, and yet I don't *make* myself do it. My ultimate laziness....

✳

(My mother) just doesn't like having to realize that she is getting older. I find it so sad that she has nothing to believe in — except crumbling politics and friends. She really depended on her work to keep her going — not qualitatively but just as a structure, a meaning to her life. Now that is gone and there is little to replace it.

✳

I am so unused to people saying "you" and actually meaning me — as opposed to (my husband) and me — that I hardly recognize it any more... I suppose it's another manifestation of feeling others neglect "me" when I do it myself all the time. I must pursue my biography more consciously so that I find connections, hold onto some conscious awareness of the present and conscious development into the future.

*

Added on the top of the first page of a long, sad letter was this:

"Following pages depressing to me — if will depress you, why not just throw it away without reading and yet retain the thought that I am communicating with you."

Lying here, I hate my soft white body. There is so much of it. It never sees the sun so it is embarrassingly white. I'd call it "Guilty White." How can anyone hate themselves? It's wrong to be so negative. It almost seems a thing against God. If we are not to judge one another, then the same goes for ourselves. So I sin and lie all the time to God. I ask to live more time so that I might diet and become less self-concerned and more physically able to relax — by being thin — and then more able and capable of carrying out whatever it is I am to do here… I almost feel my needs are strangulating me in anger and frustration at me for not acknowledging them, and acting on and for them. It's like wanting to burst out from isolation, but realistically knowing that life is one-step-at-a-time — one stage at a time — one person or group of people at a time, one experience and rendering at a time, waiting, working, silent and active — waiting—working-waiting-working, acknowledging, holding, accepting, working, waiting… I am so chronically, disgustingly and repetitively involved with <u>myself</u> that it is making me <u>sick</u>.

✳

I wish I knew so much, and I don't know anything really, and I'm mostly too lazy to even get on with trying to develop myself. The whole process of trying to become conscious is really so very difficult. When I think how blithely I looked at anthroposophy (spiritual science) in the beginning, I have to laugh. Knowing about it all certainly doesn't make life any easier — and yet it can give one many new perspectives. In any case, there doesn't seem to be any turning back from it anymore — at least for me.

✳

Spent most of the day talking with my mother. She is so sad and in a sense defeated. She has cut herself off from most people — so her emotions wouldn't show through — i.e. that she cares and needs people. The old tough façade, but when I would protest against it, she would begin to cry. I really am sorry for all she has had to go through. If only she would go into it a little and try to understand more but as she said, she wishes she could "get on a sailing boat and sail and sail and never have to find myself." I hope we can help her to be less troubled and bitter. She still has so much to give to people if she will only let herself.

✳

We have a study group once a week where we are talking about 'threshold phenomena' — i.e. experiences which in some way take one into the spiritual world. We feel that this isn't something that happens one day with a flash of light, etc, but that one has threshold experiences all the time and we must only learn to become more conscious of them. For instance in anger one can feel a kind of 'force' or 'possession' which comes into oneself or into the other, or in fear, or also in many positive emotions. Or sometimes you feel really connected to some idea or 'truth' and you know that it isn't the words you have heard that make the connection — or the goose bumps or the shaky feeling — you know it is more than the mere words. If only we could know more about that 'more than' and learn to see it clearly and follow it.

I did perhaps talk a bit much at a recent group — though I'm not sure of this. Certainly, I did crack a few too many jokes. I am aware sometimes half way in or immediately after but *why* do I start? I should also be more composed, more patient, less jumpy about wanting to say something and therefore grabbing time and space.

How can I *live* what I believe, interact the way I feel one could and should?

✳

I want to know more about myself... and be a mirror to others — in honest, open, caring ways. . . . How can I learn to take others into my being with real care, love — responsibility to see the best — i.e. what they are trying to be.

✳

Have I ever told you about the Thursday night group we have? There are eleven of us and we began wanting to explore how a group can/could help individuals on their own paths of development. We have done different things over the months, but the last three weeks we did a kind of exercise where one person is addressed by everyone else with their answers to three questions: 1) What do you especially appreciate about this person? 2) What would you like to give this person? — not necessarily that you yourself have, and 3) What would you like this person to throw away? I can't tell you how powerful an exercise this turned out to be — in so many ways. We all experienced an incredible caring by the others as they spoke to us — to say nothing of the many helpful things that were said. But what really surprised me was the change in my own attitude toward the others as I thought about them — during the week — and spoke to them — I really cared for them in a totally new way. Instead of judging, or being annoyed or bothered, I began to feel as if I became a part of their lives — in some small way responsible to their individual developments. As

I felt some link in caring, I could no longer just criticize but wanted to help — and most of all to understand the struggles the others are going through. The whole exercise has really given me quite a new perspective — and in a way a very useful kind of tool with which I can try to stop myself as I am being so critical and <u>try</u> to enter into the being of the other — not for my sake, but for his or hers. Of course, this is all very hard to apply in 'reality' but still it does seem to have real possible value.

✳

Is a crystal beautiful *because* it is imperfect? Does imperfection in this sense take one out of the specific thing and remind one of the process between nothing and perfection? — between reality and the spirit?

Why are we human beings? What are the archetypal perfections? Can we perceive and conceive them — and still be human? Or is that another step — and now we aspire to them as we are able.

✳

How can I develop a waiting, patient attitude without losing my directness? I must bring more warmth, caring into my perceptions and actions. This really is the old feminine/masculine balance again — within me.

✳

We had a long conversation recently on warmth — and women — and marriage. It is difficult to work out the tensions of being — wanting to be — conscious in a relationship and wanting to work to make it grow, and yet still have some illusive quality of warmth — femininity — difficult to know quite what to call it... I can no longer act out of an unconscious instinct of warmth and maternal feeling, etc — that doesn't seem to be what I am all about — and yet I do want to acquire it in some transformed way. But how — and what?... Surely 'warmth' is something basic my life is about this time — that's not the right word though — a real selflessness is part of it — an openness and involvement with others that comes across as support and caring. With some people, I can feel this beginning to come from me but so often I seem to be aloof, or critical — detached. I wonder so much about this — I have always felt that some part of me was not involved in important moments — that is, a bit back, a bit apart. Perhaps this is right — some core of objectivity, but I'm not sure. Perhaps it is all defense and protection — but of what? — fear or insecurity. Over the years, I guess many people have thought of me as 'cool' — 'removed' — I must try to explore this a bit and see how much it has been the case.

Perhaps this is connected to my feelings about some rigorous mental, analytical training in some previous life, which would appear to link me to a whole group of my friends — none of us have an instinctive femininity. But what *can* we develop now as women? — we have not chosen to be women for nothing. I feel this so strongly and with such an internal feeling of faith that I must persevere... this is a very real impulse — it must yet emerge more clearly and I must find the forms to let it grow fruitfully and helpfully — to myself and others.

I am trying not to be judgmental and critical. There are certainly enough things we don't agree on — or more specifically ways of doing things. But [my visiting mother] is trying and I am too, so hopefully things will work out. I have to not let myself be annoyed when she puts every word she hears (in the language spoken where daughter is living) into some relationship with Spanish — the only foreign language she knows — or when she compares everything with 'our' way — i.e. the American way. It's hard for me to understand how one can look at the world from such a totally self-centered point of view — I don't mean 'selfish' but that somehow her life and her experiences are the standard and point of reference for the rest of the world. Of course, everyone is this way to some extent. Or maybe it's my problem that I don't see myself as the center of existence, nor do I have a strong sense of 'roots' and a strong identification with places I have lived. Anyway, I feel I am unfair to her when I let this part of her bother me — but it still does bother me.

*

I really feel one must try so hard to live into the present —
without recriminations or great praises on the past and fears
or illusions for the future.

*

I am <u>determined</u> to begin to try to think more disciplinedly
— I really mean it. God — I am so aware of what a sham-
bles my mind is — I have a picture of it like a cement mixer
— stuff constantly being shoveled in and swilling around
and around and getting all mixed up together and hope-
lessly confused. It is <u>will</u> and we <u>must</u> exercise it.

*

I've been thinking about — how do I think?
- randomly — sanguinely — reactively
- in dialogue — most creative way for me — gives me
  input. I can be quite — too? — clear, logical
- by writing — a kind of dialogue with self — ideas come
  as my pen moves — hard to just sit and think without
  writing — things evaporate

I feel full of many un-thought-out thoughts — i.e. I get
many quick insights, snatches and leave it there, feeling I
'know' whatever — I resist thinking everything out. With
questions — I sometimes feel as if the answer lies in the

question and that is enough. I resist the final answer or conclusion — leave it, as it were, unsaid.

✳

What (my mother) has really shied away from, hidden — as a child — been afraid of, covered up and otherwise avoided confronting is her own self. Then at 63 — when that self could be freer[2] if she would only let it — she was literally stripped of all the externals that supported her — job, apartment, control of free movement by the accident, declining general health and on and on. It's almost as if her situation was trying to force her to confront herself and see where to go next. But she doesn't want to — and that is what is so sad. She is bitter and hurt that everything has fallen away — which is understandable — but she doesn't believe that there is really anything left inside. Or at least right now she doesn't feel the fight to find that something is worth it. She uses the old quote about "the mask becoming the face" — and it's true in a way — but she even believes it <u>should</u> be that way. Or at least a part of her does — out of habit.

---

2   Here the writer is referring to the idea, coming from Rudolf Steiner, that after 63 we are in a sense freer of our karmic duties — or one could say, of the intentions for this life that we brought over from the spiritual world. As this line of thinking goes, after 63 we have met these intended opportunities and challenges and while they will, of course, have ongoing consequences, we are nevertheless freer to develop ourselves more toward the future. References: ibid.

It's clear that she never really expressed her emotions through most of her life. She was too proud, and also too defensive for her mother, to do it as a child. She had to 'make it' as a young woman and always be 'strong,' never 'weak.' Perhaps (my father) never really understood her hidden moods — how could he anyway when she didn't? But she let herself go on always having — or believing she was having — a 'fun' life — and maybe pushing all questions and doubts away. After he died, she still had to maintain an image, and be strong and make it. Now there is less of an external world (i.e. job) to conquer and she is forced to look in. It is <u>so</u> hard for her to talk about real things, about herself in a non-story way but rather at a feeling, present level. She said she has <u>never</u> been as open as with us — and yet she is so terribly tight and afraid. It's so hard to know how to really help her. And looked at from the other side, it is also hard having her always with us. I would like to be all loving, and understanding, and big enough to not be bothered by her idiosyncrasies and her presence. But I am not, and so it is hard. I don't like her dependence on me, from the little things — like, "Will you ask (my husband) to empty the garbage" — to the big things — like what to do with her day, her month, her life. I keep feeling that for her sake she would be better off living on her own and having her own life to be interested in. And I admit I would prefer to have my own life too. It's all so complicated.

*

Somewhere in the last five years, both my parents and their lifestyle have lost their capacity to threaten me, a discovery which surprises and overjoys me. My mother, too, seems to have been able to come to some sort of agreement with herself about "letting bygones be bygones" as she would say, and is less tense than she's been around me for years. Maybe vice versa is also true? In fact, so far, it is even pleasant! If I sound cautious and it seems unnecessarily, I guess it's just that I'm scared it can't last, though there's no reason why it shouldn't, I guess. My father is, as usual, locked in his own world… We are finding it possible to talk honestly, even if in a fairly low key way, with my mother about Anthroposophy and bio-dynamics. She is utterly non-committal, and if I pressed her at all, I expect she'd say "It's your life" — but she <u>does</u> listen — and in some things — e.g. companion planting, herbal medicine — is very receptive… She humors me — not without sarcasm — re: (the baby) and TV, radio, non-synthetics, etc — though I think she's longing to point out we can't be too extreme or we'll make her a freak. Today she drew some superficially not totally unwarranted comparisons between our witnessable behavior and that of Exclusive Brethren. I laughed at her and told her firmly not to be ridiculous — thinking who am <u>I</u> kidding? — and my grandmother said — "<u>Of course</u> she wouldn't be an Exclusive Brethren" with such conviction that they all shut up. Thank you, grandmother, I breathed, where did <u>that</u> come from?

*

1976 – 1977

What is serenity? — waiting in peace, having a living perspective, valuing each moment, breathing rhythmically. We forget to be serene — and then get in a panic for it. How to let it envelop us? — but not as if asleep.

*

I don't know *why* turning 28 should seem *so* significant to me, apart from the obvious seven yearness, but it does. Notwithstanding the significance, I spent the day cleaning chicory and now must mop and polish the kitchen floor (well, it's a small kitchen, thank God), and do the washing up and so on. Ah me.

*

(A friend) spoke of 'information' working through in her thoughts and in her relationship — now more 'consciously.' This made me realize how much the group has helped me make conscious so many things that have lived — swimmingly — within me. But also through the group I feel my consciousness has been 'warmed', made 'softer' — in my relationship I feel this strongly, but also in my 'critical' ways — now I feel more able to work up to things rather than plunge in with my 'insights' which often hurt people — whether that was my intention or not.

*

I've been pondering feeling-thinking versus analytical-thinking — I need the development of both — creative thinking which includes both.

*

Of course, one learns many ways of being intuitive with another — overtime. Still I have this compulsion to make so many things conscious — as if — in fact — they will not be understood — by ourselves or the other or both? — unless they are clearly articulated.

*

Why do I ask so many questions and not *answer* them? Is it fear of in-depth thinking? — Fear of form, or contraction, of drawing a conclusion? Surely it must be, but *why*? Is this lack of confidence really a feminine trait? — not taking oneself seriously as a thinking, creative person.

*

What is concentration? — entering into the moment, discipline, finishing something, thought, order. . . . So many things come in — children, phone, many-ness of household tasks, friends... How aware am I of what I am doing at any moment? — i.e now I am writing, slouched on the couch, my ear itches, I hear birds, and I wonder how much 'free' time I have left... I would like to be more fully *in* whatever I am doing, *but* I also value that I can do more than one thing — it drives me crazy that (my husband) cannot talk and do the dishes! *But* when I want to concentrate, I cannot — I am prey to sense impressions, thoughts, memories, etc. How can I learn to sit for a moment in empty silence? to *wait* in peace for what might come. That is concentration on nothing, but also how can I develop a discipline in concentration — to follow through seriously what I intend — rigorously and with some order?

✳

How to develop an understanding sense of self — that allows perspective, wholeness, to show in one's daily life? — purpose, spiritual task, love, confidence, joy in the moments — including (my husband), friends, work, study, reading, quiet moments, nature.

✳

My parents and grandmother have been with us since about the 19th of December, and it's proving an interesting and often rewarding experience — can you hear the echoes of amazement? Of course, it's not always either of those things! But it's the first time they have visited us, in a space of our own, where we both feel comfortable and complete. And we have been able to let what's around us speak for us, and I think we have sometimes really met each other. I have also made conscious — to myself — the nature of a lot of the pressure I feel when I am around my mother... and it has made it easier to deal with. Where before, I used to just resent the intrusion upon my self, my will, my being, I feel now a sort of directionless superabundance of caring coming from her, and such a <u>need</u> to be able to care; I have been really trying to make the space for that to be freely there, such a struggle with so many parts of myself. Both my mother and my father have been able to grow into being grandmother and grandfather, too, in this time — it's an incredible relief to see it finally sitting comfortably upon them.

*

What does wholeness mean? Is it a question of *perspective*? — i.e. something that encloses, makes whole one's total being. In this sense, how can a scattered day be redeemed, seen in its value: flexibility, openness — to possibilities, to others, to dangers, to moments, to joys — responsibility and caring. But what of the tiredness — actual and psychological — the feeling of nothing to show for a day gone by, the loneliness in the midst of hullaballoo, the seeming endless repetitions, the inner dreams, the feeling of slipping — out of the world, away from thoughts, adults — the need for self-nourishment.

※

How did I relate to being a woman? I sensed no limits in childhood — I could do anything and received parental and school support for this. I valued my intelligence and my other — social — side but although they had links, they were in many ways two worlds — especially in terms of friends. What in this was connected to sensing myself as woman — in a way of putting aside my intelligence in social situations? It was a dilemma that became clear as I went into graduate school — the dilemma of some intelligence *and* some looks — one or the other seemed easier.

But in marriage real *woman*hood came with pregnancy. Suddenly all the limitations, and I didn't know what I wanted. I couldn't deny motherhood but wasn't prepared for it. Suddenly I was a 'wife' — not so much in roles but in identity. I felt the loss of old identities and a lack of connection to that new one. Also a loss of confidence as I felt I was 'seen' less — not conscious then in me. This finally moved into the question of what is it to be a woman? What did I intend in the spiritual world and how is that intention working through in life? How can we know this intention? With more consciousness of womanhood, I went into a partly superior, patronizing phase. This is now more balanced.

※

The point where I am stuck in myself is that I demand from the 'outer world,' the others (my husband) to make space for me. I expect others to notice me or to offer me something. I haven't learned to <u>ask</u> or to <u>take</u> just in a natural way. When I do now I mostly am cross, disappointed, etc. — I feel it as a real personal trouble, and I see, too, that the way I look at women's questions is through this problem. I recognize that many, many women are struggling with this problem, and so I make my problem into an objective question of freedom. And probably this is the truth, but still I feel I must work first on my own problem.

∗

Masculine-feminine inner balance — If within we can feel where we are acting from, we can be clearer... Maybe we need to get away from too early value judgments — i.e. that's good and masculine, or good and feminine.

∗

I am *so* tired. (My husband) does the evening milking, and we eat after that and it's always nine by the time we're finished, and it's about all I can do to be present at the washing up, and then I collapse into bed. And 10-6 should be enough sleep, but I have such ridiculous, incredible dreams which constantly wake me up, that I probably don't get as much sleep as I should. All this sounds so complaining. I don't really feel that way — just being driven out of my mind by all the things I don't have time and energy for. I decided long ago that this particular crisis is purely a matter of standards and that mine are too high, but recognizing that doesn't help me *really* deal with it. I try to be 'more efficient' but (the baby) absolutely ensures that efficiency is out of the question — probably just as well! — so I've pretty much given up that one, except in short bursts.

*

And where in all this does our SPIRITUAL DEVELOP-MENT stand? Well might you ask. I keep thinking I *must* get up at 5 am instead of 6 am and then just GROAN. I simply haven't got it in me at the moment to do it. EVER? I dunno. It's easy to blame things on pregnancy.

*

Is the connection of the exercises to the days of the week a real connection in itself or merely a way to go about the eight-fold path[3] in a rhythmic, harmonious, regular way? —

---

3   In discussing the Eight-fold Path Rudolf Steiner brought a connection of this work to the different days of the week, named as they are after the evolutionary planets. Many people have found it useful to work with these daily invitations to strengthen different aspects of our consciousness: Sunday — Right Judgment; Monday — Right Word; Tuesday — Right Deed; Wednesday — Right Livelihood; Thursday — Right Endeavor; Friday — Right Memory; Saturday — Right Thought; and then the eighth — Right

i.e. Do we do it because the day changes help us to become clear of all the steps, or because a specific exercise *belongs* to a day? I can see a valuable use of the exercises in giving an over-all structure and meaning to the week — beyond merely daily tasks.

*

How to bring order — non-rigid — into one's surroundings and one's day? — greater patience — inner calm, not to let emotions rise — avoid patterns of reaction to children, (my husband) or myself. Generally I must breathe easier — plan and execute more carefully — learn to say "no" — to others and to self-diversions and indulgences — have everything in better *order*.

*

(In terms of developing more order/self-discipline) how do you relate to these suggestions I am thinking about:
- Stop — in a moment to break a destructive pattern — breathe, remember a verse or an exercise or an intention, then enter the situation again
- begin the day with some (worthy) thought

Examination — serves as a looking back on the whole week. For a further elaboration of the Eight-Fold Path, see Rudolf Steiner's *How to Know Higher Worlds. The Eight-fold Path* is also sometimes referred to as the path of the Buddha.

- consider what the day will hold — in the morning or the night before
- review the day (before sleep)
- find a few quiet moments
- try to do some things with a regularity of time — i.e. flowers, beds...
- touch nature somehow
- avoid panting through a day

✳

I'm more interested in 'being' than 'doing'... in a basic sense of first priorities. I took time to see it this way — i.e. anguish of 'what will I do' and suddenly realizing 'I am' — and out of that I will do — more or less consciously at different times. *When* I need to work on my 'direction' I need to call on my more *masculine* traits of clear thinking, logic, planning, etc, but if I'm not engaged in my 'being,' the direction doesn't *go* anywhere.

✳

We have begun a weekly group again with the hope of supporting each other in real development, inner discipline, acceptance... We said last time — two weeks ago — we would work on the question of acceptance — of what is in our lives, relationships, etc. Trying at times to be aware of this, gives me a more phlegmatic approach — or patience? — to just live something through, controlling the emotional turmoil which would actually *be* irrelevant.

But what of justifiable — can it be? — anger, disappointment? i.e. (my husband) not giving a message — he was, of course, very sorry — *how* could I react? What learn? How overcome? or (my child) breaking the recorder — or hitting/kicking in blind anger.

*

In relation to an exercise in Steiner's *Reincarnation and Karma,* I had an amazing experience — trying to "live into" something from which I had once extricated myself. I thought of graduate school and began to imagine earnestly wanting to be in that world, doing research, caring about footnotes, articles, etc. I pictured a seminar I remembered finding so ludicrous and wanted to build an interest — small one — that I could get passionately/intellectually into. Warning myself against caricature I decided I wanted to explore the transition in English into a *neuter* article — *the* — out of masculine/feminine in other languages. Then — light bulb! — of course that is *fascinating* to me now. Why in the language of (our times) — English — should this 'neuter' come in — in terms of the whole evolution toward some future androgyny?

I've never thought of this before and probably wouldn't have — but it might be important — really a gift idea.

*

1978 – 1980

I should mention something that has really HIT me in the last few months. It's so good that it's finally become <u>true</u> for me, every time I remember that I know it now, I feel happy. And it is, that there is <u>time</u> in my life for a variety of things, that I do not have to achieve <u>everything</u> today, yesterday or tomorrow. And in fact, that there are some things that <u>have</u> to wait, because I won't be able to do them til I'm in another age place. Well, sounds very obvious, doesn't it, but I can assure you I've never <u>really</u> known that until now. It began to dawn in me as I watched myself and our emerging play group and saw with surprise — and satisfaction, I guess — that I was doing lots of stuff effortlessly that at other times in my life I'd found so enormous as to be almost impossible. I kept thinking, but I don't <u>like</u> organizing people. And then realizing I was enjoying myself. Perhaps it's also that I'm doing it differently and better and it's easier! However, as all this went on, I gradually saw that if I can do this at 30, maybe there's something else I can do at 40 that I couldn't do at 30 and so on. What a <u>blast</u> that was!

＊

I seem to have concluded a very patchwork sort of year. Many activities and involvements but no independent pattern has emerged from any one thing. Am I any closer to some real answers? For all my doing and working with others I despair so often over my true inner path. As if nothing deepens, all is sanguinity and I'm basically at the mercy of my moods. My trip was an incredible high because everything flattered my little ego — I was independent, capable, young, attractive, humorous, fluent — or so people made me feel, and yet here, once the rush was over, I'm just me again: mother of two kids, struggling wife, unvital, unattractive, unnoticed! I'm exaggerating of course, but do you know what I mean? And where is that inner shining light that should transcend both realities? It seems so undeveloped. I have so many questions and interests, I read endless biographies, diaries, life and destiny experiences, human wisdom. I write a diary and try to understand what it's all about. Or rather what are all the <u>details</u> about. The big things seem clear. Love is essential and Christianity really, but what do I do — here — and how and when? How much do I respond to what is asked of me and how much do I carve something new. I suddenly feel terribly creative: I want to sing all the time, I want to act, I want to write. Why now, when I have no time of my own and little opportunity?

✳

How much can we need each other? Is this the lesson for me? Have I wrongly needed (my husband), have I wanted more than I should — more than is right? I do feel he should have reached to me, that he should have known the depths of my plea.

In my semi-madness, I (just) heard wisdom in the radio of some neighbors blaring through the woods. I had tried blocking my ears with no luck, didn't want to relinquish my desire for sunshine and so resolved to endure such 'modern' disturbance to my own — selfish — wish for silence. Next song: "When I'm feeling all alone, Mother Mary comes to me, speaking words of wisdom, let it be..." And then they turned it way up so it reverberated through the garden and through me — "Let it be, let it be — there will be an answer, let it be"... There is an answer in it somewhere for me. Since that song, there has been no more music.

＊

(My three-year-old) was very impressed by your number of years, when I told her it was your birthday and that you would be 33. Not that it means anything to her... Your birthday, how was it? Are you having a midlife crisis yet? Ever since I read *Passages* a couple of years ago, I've been awaiting mine with baited breath. Got a feeling mine won't be in the form of coming to terms with my mortality — I fell off a bike too many times when I was learning to ride — I've done that one. I don't mean to disparage the book. I thought it was very good. By the way, have you read — you must have — *The Women's Room*? What did you think? I <u>loved</u> it. Wish I could talk to you, I hate unanswered questions.

＊

I smile at your question of do I get time to be myself. I truly don't know. I struggle for moments of peace only to find I'm too exhausted to do as much with them as I want to! I <u>do</u> achieve a lot, and I don't feel any sense of being diminished by children. But I never do as much as I want to, or even as much as I think I will and that constantly shits me. I've given up lusting after time alone. About three weeks ago, two friends arrived here one morning and announced they were taking all three children for the day — till 5:30 pm. I have not had one day <u>entirely</u> to myself since (the oldest) was born. I couldn't believe that, when I thought it, and here I was in an <u>empty</u> house, <u>alone</u>... I hardly knew where to start — didn't know whether to lie on the bed and read all day, or sew in peace, without (the baby) pushing the foot control and running the needle through my finger and (the oldest) saying, "I want to sew. You <u>never</u> let <u>me</u> sew. You are mean", etc. and (the second) saying "Why does that lever go down there?" and pulling at it to see. It was a wonderful day — I couldn't thank them adequately. Living near one's parents, <u>would</u> have some advantages! The only way (my husband) or I can get time away is for the other of us to mind the kids. I'd love a baby-sitter — but they're difficult to come by, especially for three children — because <u>I</u> know what it's like to look after them, I can't with a clear conscience ask anyone else unless I really have to.

*

(My husband) and I are reading *Karmic Relationships*, Vol I (Rudolf Steiner) together which of course relates to all these 'biography' questions I have been wondering about. It's an amazing series of lectures — always leaving me spinning with more questions. I then want to talk them all out — and all those which come up along the way! — while (my husband) gets sleepier... I wonder if I need to talk for my questions or if I waste them sometimes by talking... but also I forget many I don't talk through. It is clear that I 'think' better in conversation and I wonder why this is. The dialogue can of course be internal, or on paper, but it still most often takes the form of a dialogue.

✳

How much of a (negative) critical approach can come from upbringing/education but not be central to one's being? and so can be sloughed off with age — and effort? A lot I think! — hope?!

✳

What does it mean to be too concerned about right and wrong? — to be too black and white? I have no desire to be grey — however it might be good to round off my sharper edges.

✳

Difficult feelings with (my mother). She can be so shallow,

and self-centered, and even mean — but she doesn't know it. So why do I get so upset? Sometimes it bursts out, other times shows in a stiff kind of coldness/removal — but always it eats into my insides. And I feel guilty that I feel sometimes so critical of her. But can't she be happy for (my sibling about to get married)? Is there no way she can <u>really</u> feel the wonder of it all — and truly wish them well? Of course, she does wish them well — but inside there seems to be such inconsistency and tension — and jealousy (?) I yearn to be able to help her with this — and instead I get angry. Why is their (my mother and my sibling) relationship so very tortured? Is there no way to pierce this veil?

*

We talked about death, reincarnation, karma. I spoke of how I don't see a pattern of reincarnations as essentially a personal path — i.e. for personal/self-advancement — struggle — progress. A world of only that kind of self-development makes no sense to me — there must be more we are all to do — as human beings evolving with and for the Earth. This really does live in me, yet it isn't obvious to others and that is hard for me to understand. I don't think I ever have thought of reincarnation as a means to personal gain, <u>or</u> as a crutch, <u>or</u> as an escape for things of this life — but how do others think it would be about such things?

*

How can I really learn to listen into phenomena? — into myself? — into world events? Listen to the true spirit calling. "We people of today need a true ear for the spirit's awakening call…" **(from a verse by Rudolf Steiner)**

✳

It's strange how the whole subject (of moving) seems out of the realm of desire/want-not want… I don't 'want' to go — yet still it's there. What is our 'freedom' here — in the face of feeling it's inevitable? We have tried to penetrate it with our consciousness — but it isn't a question of what we like/want. What really is in store?

✳

1981 – 1982

(A friend) came for the evening. He spoke of a 'network' of one's community which suddenly becomes visible as one prepares to leave a place. I thought — is this a kind of experiencing of one's etheric (life force) — all the interweaving which forms your life structure? It makes sense to me. If pain is connected to experiencing the border of something — i.e. becoming aware of your skin — then this is also what is happening as your particular life structure becomes disturbed — there is pain as the perimeter becomes evident/ as the area contracts.

I Give You My Word

*

I have almost finished Volume I of *Karmic Relationships*. I also brought Volume II with me on holiday. I don't know why I haven't read them before, but it definitely feels the right time to work on this area. You have read Vol I & II haven't you? Reading the lectures, I find — like I do with all of Steiner's work — a kind of meditation, close to what lives deepest and truest in me. It gives me strength and wakes me up. Somehow I plan to take up Karma and Reincarnation as "my theme" for the year. — This is said almost in a whisper, because I know too well how easy it is to say — how big it sounds — how hard to keep up. Of course, it will be after and in between all the other tasks and responsibilities and projects. But I have made a kind of inner resolve to do some real work, both reading and also doing some exercises. I feel it's always been behind and central to the work our group has done together, although we never actually came to it directly — or not very often.

*

Already again I meet in myself the need to learn to <u>trust</u>. So often, especially when it comes to sharing responsibility, delegating, etc, I find myself not trusting. And in business transactions like selling cars. Not, I don't think, in my personal relationships — and I never had that with you. It's so depressing to know all the inner work is waiting to be done, as well as the outer. I'm so lazy and spend so much energy worrying about what I have to do — inner and outer — instead of getting on with it. Do you think there is any hope for me?

*

To get back to inner life... I'm struggling to get to work and feel like you said <u>NOW</u> is the time. At the end of work days, (a colleague) read the Foundation Stone (**a long meditation given by Rudolf Steiner at the founding of the Anthroposophical Society in 1923**) and afterwards I wept in the car <u>because</u> in the face of what is my deepest wish and intention, I feel myself so inadequate and so far away. Sometimes if I look at my life, I can't see how I got here and how it is that this 'spirit striving' — I don't know what to call it — is so strong in me. I was just an ordinary kid doing all the typical American things, middle class America... Nothing external really brought me here — except of course my own two feet and various significant meetings and experiences. . . . It just surprises me to see and find myself here sometimes. It's also that feeling of being so small and having such a long way to go, yet somewhere in the center and depth, I'm there. So why don't I get on with it?...In small ways I'm trying to get on with it. (My husband) and I are trying to get into a rhythm with the 8-fold Path. It's good work when it happens and I try not to despair when it lapses but just pick it up again when I remember. Also with the 'Ruckschau' *(daily review),* and just generally observing and working on what are sometimes some painful revelations of how far I have to go. I try to listen, inwardly silent, receptive, waiting, not quick to speak, but I get so excited about what someone is saying that I can't stop my thoughts bubbling up and a response bursting out... Or, how can I make a resolve to pay attention to my impatience and anger and half an hour later find myself totally caught up in those very emotions? So I plod on. I too have been reading *Knowledge of Higher Worlds*, **(by Rudolf Steiner; the title in recent editions is translated into English as *How to Know Higher Worlds*)** and I'm loving it. It somehow feels so soothing, such a comfort, and I feel very stirred inwardly by it.

I hope it's not too long before you find your work in Detroit and with it, your friends. Because of the other pressures on our lives, I think that it's only through working with people at one thing or another that we can develop friendships at this age, and that is one of the frustrations of my life at the moment, I think. However, I <u>really</u> know that if I am patient enough, at the right time, something <u>will</u> present itself that I can do — it's wondering how long it will take that gets me down sometimes! I just hope that it doesn't take too long to heal the etheric wounds of parting — after that time in England, it's bound to be, for people and for place — and in my experience it unfortunately heals <u>slowly</u>.

I'm sorry if our call upset you.... Maybe it's better to trust in our thoughts bringing us close to each other. You sounded so sad, all through our talk, yet the insistence of the telephone and the distance made it so impossible to ask about all the levels of that sadness. But now I just feel helpless and sorry and want to send you all the love and embracing thoughts I can.

. . .

I don't want to be constantly pulling you back. I don't feel in my heart that I am; at least I don't intend to do so. But how can we let our relationship grow in new ways without clinging to the past but being open to the future... I didn't know you the first year you were here, but remember how difficult it was, and even after that... And remember how difficult you found our group that first year, left alone in it without (the co-founder)? You might not have been able to predict how close we would all grow to one another, the work that would unfold for you, the love that would grow between you and so many people. But it did. We can only see such small sections of time, but I'm sure there is much there for you now, ready to unfold that you can't see yet. It's obviously there or you wouldn't be there. Plus you've got all our hearts with you....

＊

I sometimes wish I just <u>was</u> and didn't continually have to strive to become!

176

＊

You say you're still lonely, but you have accepted it. I would do anything to help you over it, but I also know that you are strong enough to work at it. In Forest Row, it is easy to cover up lots of things with a thousand activities and in crowds of nice people. But this doesn't help in the search of some inner peace, a 'thing,' a treasure I am very much after at the moment. To know that many of us have that same struggle, even if they are thousands of miles away, that helps.

＊

Finally, after practically having to tie it round my neck, I've been working my way through *Occult Science* (**by Rudolf Steiner, now translated in English as *An Outline of Esoteric Science***). I can't believe how deeply it moves me, and how little I move, and how much more it means to me now. But even now, re-reading a paragraph a half an hour later because I could not remember where I had left off, I find new things in the same paragraph — different things stand out each time.

＊

I think I could lecture on the effects of an unrhythmic life — <u>from my experience</u>, but how can I speak about rhythm, breath, flow when mostly I can't breathe for fear, or anxiety, or indigestion and disorder! Help.

✳

One thing that became clear for me from the conference is that we are not doing anyone any good by taking on a thousand activities but neglecting real inner work, and that inner work needs time, like everything else.

✳

I struggle with a very intense feeling of being thrown back on myself, feeling the limits of skin and bones, not much grace around me. Having to make so many things happen in a new way, a way that I'm sure depends on my inner activity. Also — and this will sound almost pretentious written so please unfix it for me — I do find I meet my shadow, unredeemed sides, all the time. I guess I've never been one not to see the muck, but somehow now they — it? — are almost personified beings and harder to shut the door on, or to 'turn over a new leaf'. But I don't want to shake hands with them either. Should I? I growled at some disgusting little thing the other day and that definitely seemed to help. This may sound comical, or mad, but I'm serious and not yet mad — but depressed at the moment. Anyway, it calls for 1) you to talk to, which to my constant grief and frustration I cannot do in the way that I long for, and/or 2) inner work which my heart always intends and my head knows is needed but my will too, too often remains unengaged. Why?! Also I feel something like you said you do — I long to withdraw, to turn inwards and yet I am more extended, responsible for more things than ever. Yet I can't do any of them properly anymore without another kind of work, but the outer work leaves me exhausted and feeling that there is no time — or that I am a hopeless case anyway — and so I go round and round.

❋

I feel I need to learn to keep things alive and let them grow and develop on my own. I feel too, more and more, this is a time for aloneness, inwardness, even loneliness — and silence?! — and withdrawal — in some ways — after so many years of rich exchange and friendship. I do know this time totally belongs to me, is part of my destiny, so when will I stop complaining?

❋

In the following and several later excerpts there is reference made to the Moon Node — another archetypal period in a life journey that several writers were experiencing and then commenting on. Briefly, the Moon Node refers to the roughly 18½-year rhythm that reflects the relationship between the earth, the sun and the moon at the time of one's birth. The First Moon Node is between eighteen and nineteen, the second one — which is what the letters address — is between thirty-seven and thirty-eight. An imagination of this recurring rhythm can be that we spiral once again past a cosmic gateway we passed through as we entered into life. Deeply held life themes and questions may resound within us, even challenging us in surprising ways. Dreams can feel especially important. The Second Moon Node, in particular, is a time when many people experience important openings and closings in relation to some of their basic life intentions.

I hope you are ok and that your birthday was good, light and forward looking. I found from my birthday — 37th — through the moon node time really a lifting, a momentary hope and a kind of a new beginning, or promise of one... of course you were here around that time, in May, so that helped . . . but anyway I hope you find something similar. I had lots of dreams too, and I'm sorry I didn't write them down. Well, it's a kind of adventure, being 37 — says the old wise one! — so blessings on your adventure.

*

I keep having very long complicated and 'deeply significant' dreams. Finally, the other night I dreamt a dream that had links with a repetitive dream I had when I was 18. And in it I found myself saying this must be significant because it is my moon node! Then I realized that all these dreams might be because of that... The dream wasn't altogether pleasant but it was very strong. I've decided to keep a dream book of this year — but since I decided that, I haven't remembered one dream.

*

1983 — 1984

I felt so sad reading your note, sad that you are — or were at that moment — down and suffering and lonely and me unable to walk in and talk. You are so vulnerable — and I think it is your blessing but also, obviously a difficulty. So how can you strengthen yourself so that things don't go quite so deep, or wound so much? I think it must be so much harder there in America where there is so little protection around, so much a lack of nurture/rhythm.

I think the loneliness, which I also have been feeling so strongly now — especially strangely, as a presence through the night and first thing on waking — will just be there along with all the rest of the good, enjoyable, annoying, depressing things that fill the days. It's just there — maybe one day it will transform into...what? — anger turns to love, and so I continue to hope.... What does loneliness turn to? — being with friends again I hope.

*

Tomorrow will bring to a close my moon node year. Looking back, I've never had a fuller year — very, very busy. Some wonderful moments... much <u>very</u> lonely perseverance and hard work, some real anguish in meeting myself and struggling in relationships, lots of wondering what is my work, more acceptance of the loss to my life that your move was/ is, more understanding, almost intimacy with the loneliness that's brought a beginning of pulling out of sadness, feeling the only way to go is forward and trust.

*

I also feel this whole time, since you and (your husband) left, the time approaching and surrounding my moon node was among other things telling me I had to stand alone, on my own two feet and give out what all those years of friendship and Ariadne and support and learning gave to me... But also I had some bonuses — at the moon node you visited — how I wish I could visit you — and the counseling weeks which felt real and mighty and made me contact that essential core and begin to rise out of the gloom of missing you.

*

I am so sick of all the old thoughts, lectures, habits, tasks. I seem to be <u>forever</u> re-creating the old. I can't bear it sometimes, yet I am asked to. Also, this feeling extends really to my whole personality structure. I'm tired of who

I appear to be. I want to tear away, layer by layer, all the habits, reactions, attitudes, ways of speaking, laughing, to find and be me. I know it's existential and archetypal, but that's where I am. Sometimes I'm caught being different sides of <u>me</u> — for instance, to two different people at the lunch table — one side gentle and understanding and deep, the other side quick, argumentative, clear and challenging — head and heart miles apart and I feel Help. Who am I?

✳

Variety is truly the spice of life and the continuation of my excessive sanguinity. In between washing and weighing vegetables, wiping bums and noses, sharpening pencils, cutting lunches, telling stories, cooking meals, washing clothes, going shopping, and being an excellent role model for all my children, these days, I also teach two hours of crafts each afternoon, and try to whole-heartedly and whole-mindedly go to one study group and one staff-meeting per week. I can <u>honestly</u> say that I think that our — my — life is totally crazy, and that if I could see any way short of a lobotomy or a coronary, to change it, I would. But it's like everything else — once you're inside the birdcage and pedaling at 1000 mph on the little wheel, it's hard to know who/where to stop.

✳

My mother now walks on 2 crutches until her second hip has healed. She is patient and in good spirits, but it still makes me sad to see the life she now leads. There is not much purpose in it — everything is so orderly and set. I try so hard to fight similar tendencies in myself, but I must accept her as she is.

*

Tell me I am arrogant and critical — I will accept it from you. I even accept it from myself — and others. But I don't believe in doing things if they aren't done well. My mother brainwashed me — I believed her in ways undreamed of by her, I am sure. Everywhere I carry this blessing/burden — two-foldness for me and also for the other... I marvel at how people don't attend to the details. Do I, should I, need I always pick those up, or can I let them drop and feel confident that if they are important someone else will pick them up?

*

Here I am in hospital — not a familiar surrounding for me — and I feel so strange, like an actress in a play, or like being awake inside a dream, even someone else's... It's been so strange and still hard to know what's up... I gather it's all about bringing rhythm into my life, concentrating my energies, saying no to what does not belong to me, etc. (My husband) says women want completeness but should not strive for perfection. Men strive for perfection but lack completeness. He says I want both — i.e. my preparing time — and that's bad. I say it's balance. Or is it?... I wonder what I'll do with (this time). Do new research? New thinking? Finally do some painting, or form drawing? Get my inner life in order? Well if this hiatus in my life is for that, and I can truly use it for that, maybe I can see some meaning in it. But if I spend it depressed or cleaning the house — help!

✳

I feel like such a blah because I have so little to share. I've been so inward, so removed from the 'outside world.' My days seem to be consumed with hospitals, tests, and doctors. You know how when you move, or re-decorate a house, how all the details take so much time and can consume all your thinking. Well, I'm caught in a similar way by symptoms and appointments. Still, in many ways my eyes have been opened — I'm back to square one — not that I ever really left it — but again realize how important it is — Control of Thinking.[4] That has been a real trial for me. It seems so 'easy'

---

4   This is a reference to the first of what Rudolf Steiner elaborated as the Six Exercises, which invite us to practice being centered in our Thinking, Will, Feeling, Positivity, Openness, and a final Harmonizing of them all. These have been described extensively, for example in: *An Outline of Esoteric Science* by Rudolf Steiner; *Meditation as Contemplative Inquiry* by Arthur Zajonc; *Stairway of Surprise* by Michael Lipson; or in my book *Why on Earth? — Biography and the Practice of Human Becoming*.

when life is going smoothly. Also, I've become so acutely aware of the suffering, and frailty of people — not now my own but of so many, many people. So I've been pondering those eternal unanswerable questions of life — of death — of destiny in general, but also with a certain urgency and particularity. Also been aware of the destructiveness of the grip of fear — and false imaginings that have an iron grip but dissolve to nothingness in a second, in the face of <u>real</u> strength. But all these things need 'conversation' to explore...

*

I feel that I am fully recovered. The last few weeks, I've felt my familiar bouncy self — I may not actually look bouncy or bubbly from outside, but inside, when I'm feeling well, there's a definite tingle, upsurge of life and enthusiasm going on a lot of the time — not always but still I can count on it — or could until I got 'ill.' Then I realized that etheric upbuilding, anti-gravity life force was not something you could always take for granted. It was — is — a grace, a mysterious blessing that needs to be respected and not stretched too thin. So... I feel the flow of life again and really for what seemed so long, I didn't feel it. Also, of course, I'm my old fat self again, though some say my face has altered — "wider cheek bones," "thinner," "softer." My own opinion is that I look a bit older and greyer.

Psychologically, too, I feel well — whole again. The anxiety and tension dispersed. My concentration returned but I haven't used it much. I haven't really 'used' this time at all. So much of my time was taken up with doctors, hospital and feeling lousy and barely coping that, until November, it was impossible to do anything. Since then, all that I can say I have done is talk to students, plan next term and summer school <u>and</u> curative eurythmy (movement). I've really loved doing that, strange as it may seem, and strange as it may be to imagine me doing it. I was pretty hopeless in the beginning, but my body remembered that there was such a thing as movement and began to move. I've found places that are stuck — have been for I don't know how long — and I've been interested to see if I could penetrate them. I hope to continue somehow next term, although I'm told I don't 'need' to — which is also encouraging. I thought for sure they would prescribe a lifetime of treatment!

It still seems for many that anthroposophy appears to make people cut out or hide feelings, to make relationships more difficult, to be cold, repressive, unjoyful, dogmatic. There is such a task there still I think: to live anthroposophy in the way it needs to be lived — with warmth and joy and openness, with true compassion and interest in the other. Why is it that people feel the heart squeezed out when the heart sphere is central to a new understanding of the human being — which is what anthroposophy is about?

＊

I am having — a Rat, in this year of the Golden Rat — a good year. Perhaps 36 is nice, after 33 and 35?? It is not without its agonies — mostly despair at my lack of knowledge and my continual 'putting off' meditative work. The world is still too much with me, and 36 is despairing that it will ever be so. Struggle for balance.

＊

I do so much want to see you in your new life, so I can share that and carry you in it in a stronger way. Although we never want, we are always too poor for holidays and travel. I long to get away, and what better place than Detroit?

＊

I wonder how you feel turning 39, your 40th year? Does it feel strange to be on the threshold of 40? I'll be glad to actually turn 40 this year, but I don't feel my inner maturity matches the outer — or rather, on another level the outer sags mirror the inner ones! Well, that's only partially true. I do feel a new strength and responsibility for my work — but still I wonder, what is my work? Anyway, what about you, how do you feel?

＊

1985 – 1987

This has so far been such a strange year for me, though it's probably wrong to say it's 'this year' as I'm sure it didn't begin at the beginning of the year. Rather, for some time now I've been conscious of being in a strange place — actually being aware of options closing — to do with age and where I'm at, and how I've voluntarily so circumscribed my life with family/work that there is no time for anything much else at all — and that's not complaint, for I really <u>like</u> my life — but statement. It's just that the awareness of how much it's so is perhaps a little scary… Will I always like it as much as I do? And even though there's a sense of options closing, there's not much sense of anything else yet opening up, though I'm sure it will. One of the things that has heightened my awareness of myself, my age, my generation, my need, the place I occupy in this life at this time, is the arrival in our midst of (a nineteen year old intern). I keep trying to convey to him how amazing it is to me that I am actually spending time speaking to a <u>male</u>, <u>and</u> a nineteen-year-old one at that!! Sounds ridiculous to write it, because I am quite aware that the kind of crazy affinity we have transcends that kind of age/generation stuff — doesn't often transcend gender though — and yet it also <u>doesn't</u>, you know. Talking with him has made me <u>so</u> aware of how much I've changed since I was 19! Sometimes I think I don't believe what this guy is saying!!

— and yet I know I thought almost the same things when I was 19... I guess one of the things that has happened is that I've started to look at my life from his perspective, and that has contained a few surprises for me... it/I look almost unrecognizable to myself! I realize the number of things that I still identify inwardly to myself as me, that outwardly I have forgone. Mostly creative stuff — no time — it's still <u>there</u>, for me — but certainly not visible to anyone else. I always think of it as something that there will be time for, again, in the future — and so have no sense of panic in the sense of temporary loss... and yet maybe that is not so. I miss painting, but I still do it in my head... so I see paintings, but the outside world sees newsletters, for example.

✳

A lot is happening, a lot is good, and yet underneath I often feel bored or like screaming. I think it's really the same old story — the outer work grows and is fulfilling but the inner? Also the outer frivolous side of life is entirely lacking...

✳

I relate strongly to your need to "define yourself as something." I can remember ruefully articulating to (a friend) years ago that I was coming to the conclusion I'd have to stay a 'light weight' — a jack-of-all-trades, master of none, forever. And I remember once you wrote to me that there wasn't anything you were doing that someone else couldn't do better. And that's a bit how I feel. And yet, I don't know that I have the devotion, the single-mindedness, to become expert in anything. I'm so sanguine. I truly despair of my sanguinity.

※

I'm deficient in future planning. I'm only OK in the present and being flexible about what's there and making the best of it. Hell. This is no time for self-awareness. At 37, it's too depressing. I wish I had the courage to answer your questions. I honestly don't know if my answer of 'don't know' is a refusal to look for a "I feel my fate, my fate finds me" *(from a Rudolf Steiner verse)*. How it seems to me, is that little by little — year by year — I feel my way through my life — now this is apparent, and then this. And that, so far, I've done what seemed to be there to be done, as it came along. Can one go on like that? I don't know. — Years ago, when someone asked me what my five-year plan was, I said — "I only have a 5 o'clock plan — if I make it through till 5 o'clock every day, I'm happy." It's not quite that bad, but nearly.

※

A new year and so many of the same intentions — for more order, rhythm, inner discipline — finding a balance between outer demands and personal needs. More and more lately I see how much I live in the <u>present</u> — respond to the moment's loudest call. It has its virtues — in fact I feel this to be one of my central life themes / goals, yet it has its problems too — lack of direction, of follow-through, of vision for the future. How do I develop more of these without losing my ability to be flexible to the moment's need? I do feel so much more aware of how this lives in me — as a general gesture and in many specific moments.

*

At the moment, I am having 4 days by myself — at a beach, in a tiny, tiny cottage which belongs to an 80-year-old friend of a friend. This is the first time in 12 years I've had time utterly and completely to myself — no conferences, no meetings, no conversations, <u>nothing</u> — except me, the sea, the rain, & SILENCE. This was the nearest thing I could find to a Trappist monastery less than an hour from (home). It's wonderful & I <u>love</u> it — tonight is the last night & I can hardly bear the thought of going back to speaking with people & cooking meals, & sweeping floors that six people have walked on, instead of one. One person doesn't make much mess, you know! I've painted some pictures & read some books & filled out my tax returns & listened to music & looked at the sea & walked along the cliff tops & it has been absolutely wonderful. I have vowed several times that I will <u>not</u> allow it to be 12 years before I have time alone again.

CHAPTER 5

Finding Ourselves — Finding Our Work

The letters show the process of self-discovery that was taking place in each of us throughout those important years in our biographies. In our different ways, we began to realize that the questions living in us were serving as growing edges guiding us toward future work in the world. For many of us the work in our women's group led to taking initiatives that encouraged others to form similar groups. Gradually those of us who had met through this work took more responsibility for what we were discovering and attempting, and we encouraged each other to offer public workshops, for example on gender-related themes. Some of us began to look at 'Motherhood' as a valued profession, needing more support in the world. Some started women's groups, parent groups, engaged in community building, or became involved in founding schools. Much of the work we did in the early days was self-created, not supported by any institutions, and mostly unpaid. And it was very exciting!

In groups and in the letters, we shared our questions and ideas — about gender and the evolution of consciousness, or feminine and masculine as qualities in all of us, or the challenge of finding balance in our daily lives. As some of us moved back to our own countries, we also began to offer workshops and courses in ever-new settings. Along the way we gave a name to this work — Ariadne, after the Greek maiden who provided a life-sustaining thread to the imprisoned hero Theseus so that he could escape from the labyrinth in which the deadly Minotaur was housed. Although Theseus soon deserted her asleep on the beach and went off to further heroic adventures, Ariadne eventually awoke, met and then married the god Dionysus, who immortalized their union by placing her crown in the night sky as the constellation Corona. Her name appealed to us because she was not an ancient all-powerful mother goddess, but a female companion figure, and even more because we felt it was time for the awakening of this feminine life-sustaining capacity in all of us, in our relationships, and in society at large. The "hero" qualities had been developing unchecked for long enough and we felt the need for a new balancing force. With this new name we started an international newsletter, offered larger conferences, and eventually some of us wrote a book called *Ariadne's Awakening — Taking up the Threads of Consciousness* (Hawthorn Press, 1986).

Some of the letters refer to Ariadne Workdays. These were international meetings that took place for several years, to share research and exercises and generally deepen the work — also, not incidentally, to let us visit with each other again. Through the work we were finding our way with language, such as distinguishing the experience of being human as a woman or a man from an automatic identification with female and male, or trying to characterize feminine and masculine as qualities in all human beings.

In addition to our interest in gender questions many other aspects of human development also called our attention, and the letters have references, for example, to life phases and temperaments. As the years went by many of us became actively involved in what would in time become known as 'biography work'. In the decades after our letters, several of us played pioneering roles in the development of professional trainings for this work in the English-speaking world.

Gradually ever more of us began working outside our homes — as teachers, farmers, adult educators, therapists, or doing whatever work would help to pay the bills. Increasingly the letters address the joys and challenges in our new working situations and the balancing acts we engaged in with our marriages and as caregivers for our growing children. Our daily lives were becoming more complicated, but in our writing we still shared ideas, hopes, experiences and support.

1974 – 1975

I want to know more about individual biography — what it means to be in the different phases — developing different bodies, soul aspects... What does it mean to be a woman — in one's own evolution, and also now in this time and society? How can a man and woman really help each other as egos?

*

I have just spent a long time on a letter to an old friend whose wife has just left him. I keep thinking about the whole problem of women — who we are? why we are? — all at so many levels. There is so much to try and understand. Somehow I feel this question is not only something I feel so very personally, but is also connected to some future work of mine. How to pursue it all rightly and consciously?

*

Single mother, just turned down for a job she applied for —

I can't believe they didn't want me. I feel I have something strong to give, but maybe I'm just fooling myself. There has to be <u>some</u> place for me — somewhere in this world. I am willing, and wanting, and anxious to do. It's so hard to keep quiet and still and wait and meanwhile always be searching and also trying to operate on a survival level, so to be healthy and around for 'those chances' when they come. Maybe my impulses are all wrong and the forces are waiting for me to come to focus. I keep trying to touch in and see if I am being selfish. Some of my wishes for good to happen to me are not perfectly 'nice' — but how do you take personality and desire and hope out of your needs? It is <u>so hard</u>.

*

It's strange for me to be back here (where I had been a student). It used to be in some sense my place — I had a reason for being here even if I had to fight hard for it. But now I am only here as a wife, and I have to fight within myself to keep how much I dislike this from bubbling over. There are so many things I would love to do here, but I really can't and so a rather complex frustration eats away at me. In some senses, I am even farther away from knowing what I want to 'do' with my life than I was a year ago. Generally, I find this a healthy step and am not upset by it but continue to plod along with some feeling of general direction. But, here there are so many tantalizing possibilities around that look of course all the better because other people are doing them and I can't be involved.

*

A friend did my astrological chart last fall. I found it really very helpful — depressing, but helpful in the sense that problems could be viewed more objectively, as things that one has to work with throughout life — really things one has chosen to work with. I found that by objectifying my difficulties this way, I could feel less guilty — perhaps not the right word — about having these problems, and so spend more energy on trying to understand and deal with them. Does that make sense? Although (my friend) tried to word it as being good in the sense of great potential for development, it was clear that I have a somewhat problem-atic chart... My problems are concerned with 'home' and sense of self — and the relation of the two. I have nothing in my work house, and, of course, this has been a great problem for me — what will I do, be, etc? In a way, it's less of a burning problem now because I feel something will come one day — when I am ready and then I will hopefully know what it is. But it's also interesting that in my chart it indicates that work will probably develop out of relationships with friends.

✳

Here's a karmic question — why be a woman or a man in a given life? What is there to learn, develop, bring through the experience? Sex sets up many 'inevitable' — planned? — struggles. My main question before was "why am I a woman now?" — in myself and society. I feel closer to understanding why in my development I chose to be a woman this time — see things I am forced/able to develop — selflessness, patience, rhythm, caring, sensitivity… I only begin to feel the emerging of 'why now,' in terms of women in society — feel there is a task to be fulfilled — ideas to be made alive, brought to others.

✳

The thought of what a new book should be — diary, thoughts on special things, journal — keeps me from beginning — that and laziness. Anyway, it's time to begin with something.

I must begin to organize my thoughts — I want to write something — perhaps on women and reincarnation.

✳

I feel a real need for realistic feedback on some of my ideas — and my ways of presenting them. I wish the group could do this for each other in time. Sometimes I get so excited as an idea is evolving in me — but perhaps it is all illusion and self-conceit.

*

1976

The need for some kind of 'mutual help' — community caring — in problems like this (relationships) seems so great — how can we rightly respond? To take this as a group question is very exciting to me.

*

What is this group? What is its importance? — i.e. *that* we meet and use our particular anthroposophical perspective. I see strongly in myself and others the excitement of what we are doing and the laziness, and fear to take it all really responsibly.

*

We work far too long for very little money, somewhat foolishly believing either a) things must change sooner or later, or b) it's 'worth' it. There are times when we query both pretty drastically... who knows what we're <u>really</u> doing? Feel as though something is <u>happening</u> but have no clue as to what, why, when. Meanwhile, it looks to all and sundry as though we're harmless fools, albeit masochistic and we are landed — ?? — frequently with 'good advice' from all kinds of people about our hours, wages — people here <u>demand</u> to know what you're earning — "What's the sugar?" is the question — and alternative places of work with better hours, wages, etc. We muddle along, telling them as much as we can in our own way.

*

What is really missing in society that must come in? This is what we must work for in ourselves, and that it can develop in others —

- Heart, soul — what do these mean in relation to the feminine?
- Isis, Mary, Sophia — who are these figures? Should we seek an archetype — with which to then relate our realities?

*

I keep thinking about the question of how women can be prepared for the problem in their thinking when with small children — i.e. sanguinity, flexibility, lack of concentration of those early years. Are there exercises one could develop? — or a perspective — how could this help? Also the question of how to move out of the void created by those years when that phase is over? I certainly feel the fear that there is nothing within me once I strip away all the excuses of why

I haven't been able to be creative, productive, etc. When the legitimate excuses go, what is left? Does it take time to replenish the void with new talents, skills, etc? How to go about this? I recognize that it's hard to grow up, to change, to move from one phase to another. Sharing in the difficulty can help one's perspective.

*

Of course... struggles must be met.... but one can have perspectives, ideas to re-consider in times of difficulty — things which can help, point to ways, take one out of one's 'uniqueness.' Is 'training' best in groups like ours? There is a need for adequate models of feminine and masculine ways — both valid and important — seeing each *other* as equal forces but appreciating the virtues of the differences.

*

What are some ways of dealing with conversations with children which allow reality and the differences of the sexes their place — i.e. a girl discusses wanting to be an actress, encourage this, talk of the discipline of the work — full-time nature, question of having a family — let her think about options. We must also find non-mother, feminine models — where the special feminine creativity is a living force in its transformed sense — perhaps working in a 'male' milieu, creations emerge from the interaction with the 'feminine' she brings.

*

We all have trouble reading — even things we really *want* to read. It can't *all* be a question of time. Might we perhaps form a study group — 1 or 2 weeks per month — to see how we exercise our thoughts? Also, we must not forget the possibility of doing something — of having some 'work' result from our group. Are we in fact re-creating the idea/ possibility/ reality of the 3-fold human being? (body, soul and spirit) — and the human soul activities of thinking, feeling and willing?

*

Here is more on thinking and the balance question — of masculine and feminine in us all — our need to become whole — have all capacities, in order to choose and have control of how one manifests in the world as a man or woman. Can we develop the possibility of clear, logical, ordered thinking without losing the intuitions we have? Do men really need to 'go away and think about that' — we, women, seem to think on our feet as it were — in the moment.

Where could we go as a group in terms of sharing our perceptions with people in need — i.e. marriage troubles. I would like to see us really exchange many ideas, possibilities and see what begins to look feasible. I have the feeling that we cannot only go on being in a way self-indulgent — we must perhaps reach out in some way… We must consider many possible forms of help — and create new ones.

*

We have had many talks about how the group can share questions with others — community center explorations, a lecture/discussion program in the fall — we all seem to be wanting to do something external though we are still unclear about quite what.

*

The question of what we are to each other continues... we seemed to all want to go deeper. It was a very tender — yet intense talk... We decided to share three questions:
- What I would like you to keep.
- What I would like to give you.
- What I would like you to throw away (be able to transform).

*

If someone wrote me out a list of THINGS TO BE ACHIEVED, I'd probably be able to begin working on it. But as it is, I feel like a blind, deaf, senseless person. I have NO IDEA where, how to begin to do WHAT? — and I hate it and it frightens me... but I don't think that's the only reason I don't want to stay here.

*

When I was reading your letter the first time and came to

the part about your thesis, it occurred to me to tell you this. Yet I don't quite know how to put it. There you are, sitting — well I know not <u>sitting</u>, but you know — <u>placed</u> in England, wondering what is my task — how best to fulfill what potential I feel I have — by the way I hate to feel you underestimate that... And it is all somehow <u>real</u> that you should have to go through this, because the 'right' thing isn't ready. It is so obvious that there is potential in the women's work, but whatever you do within this framework somehow has to be pure enough to be beyond the fragmentation that I have seen so often happen. The thesis could be very worthwhile — I ask <u>only</u> — is it <u>necessary</u> — which of course is a never ending question for me apropos of formal academic work. — I mean — is the thesis itself necessary, not the work. — As a way of publishing and perhaps spreading an idea, I can see a certain validity. I hold the question, but in no sense is it a value judgment or a criticism.

Meanwhile, by way of comparison, I smile wryly to myself about my <u>own</u> situation. What is it in my life that <u>continues</u> to provide me with necessary, menial, physical work? I almost seem to have NO choice in this — every situation in my life since I was 17 or 18, I have been thrown into unavoidable work such as I have described which leaves me no time, opportunity or necessity to wonder what I <u>should</u> do, or even what I would <u>like</u> to do. I cannot say all this utterly without resentment, and yet resentment is too strong a word, for I'm not really complaining. It seems as inevitable as shitting — maybe it's the inevitability I resent.

And really, I do wonder WHY. What do I need to learn — that I'm taking so bloody long about it — or is some kind guardian angel protecting me from procrastination or WHAT? Do tell me — I'd like to know.

✳

The following was part of a letter on behalf of an initiative group of seven women, sent to the local Waldorf school community and near-by college. Shockingly, as it turned out, over 100 women showed up for the meeting, and out of it seven new groups began. Members of the organizing group worked in pairs to facilitate these new groups. (Throughout this book there are excerpts from later letters from all of those original seven women.)

There seems to be a wish and a need to start a new group, or indeed several, to study questions especially related to women and the family. The aim is to enliven our thinking with the help of Anthroposophy and to inspire each other to bring new consciousness to old questions.

We suggest forming groups of no more than 12, according to interests and times available. If there are several groups, they could occasionally meet and exchange news of their work. Some of the many possible themes to work with are:

- Being a woman today
- Phases of development in a woman's life
- Relationships (karmic, personal . . .)
- The first 3 years of the child from the mother's point of view
- The first 7 years of the child
- The festivals with different age groups
- Wholeness and concentration in a woman's life
- Consciousness and food

I have a really thriving business started here — sell up to 20 lbs of cottage cheese as well now, as we've begun going to a 'market' about 20 miles from here, which is on Saturday morning. It's a real hotch potch of people and goods, but provided your produce is sold with reasonable respect for health regulations there seem to be not too many questions asked. We have been twice, and sold out both times — herbs are popular — in vogue — here at the minute, so fresh herb cheese has more appeal than it otherwise might. Plus, all the weightwatchers love it. What is more important to me, is that I am slowly getting locals interested, which is something! They are <u>so</u> conservative — the most conservative person in Forest Row looks like Andy Warhol compared to the least conservative here! They are still pretty dubious about the herbs — I mean it's probably <u>marijuana</u>, really, that I put in it, but they <u>will</u> try the plain one. We also started selling yoghurt, which is very much more profitable, and much less time consuming to make. I do enjoy working with food — have had lots of requests for bread since I started making a little for sale, but I can't cope with any more at the moment. It's funny though it doesn't seem 'real,' or worthwhile, in the way something less basic, more esoteric would, to me — and I realize this is kind of how I look at most of the stuff I do — yet I'd be the first to assure someone else that this practical, basic stuff is as real as the other. Maybe it's just that I feel such an imbalance in myself, knowing that the potential for 'other' work is there too — why do I only ever pursue the tangible avenues? I'm a reward seeker, when it comes down to it.

*

1977 – 1980

There is still tension to do with naming things as masculine or feminine. I feel we must — to understand and be clear about the principles — the polarity. Of course they are loaded, but that is just *why* we must get clear about them. Certainly, if I talk about them, I must define clearly my meaning at the beginning. I feel so sure of the need for a new Feminine re-emergence in society... I feel we must come to know what we are doing, wanting to do, what we must do.

*

Why we are here, in a 'cosmic' way, I have no idea. Why we are here and not somewhere else, seems to be more the question, as it's an answerable one. I think we're in the really difficult position of having no <u>good</u> reason to stay but no good reason to leave. I mean, it would be so much easier, if (our employer) suddenly turned maniacal, or the farm disintegrated, or even if he sold it… or if we were offered a job somewhere else that appealed. Would we be utterly insane — yes, but that's not a good reason not to, I know — to abandon this, in many ways good, fairly interesting, fairly learning, but utterly un<u>growing</u> — except in a purely physical sense, i.e. more skills — situation for NOTHING. The void looms. Admittedly we would be putting ourselves at the mercy of the situation and that would produce something… but what if we didn't like it? I guess what bothers me about the situation we're in now, is that <u>all</u> the good things are physical/material. We are living in a void, unrelated to anything except the children, ourselves and the farm, but it's a comfortable void… physically, not too uncomfortable mentally, a lot of the time, i.e. when I don't force myself to examine. We are — deliberately — consuming ourselves with daily life — we <u>never</u> have enough time to do all the things we want to get done and really give ourselves time, energy or space to think, anyway. Which I <u>know</u> is ridiculous and dangerous, damn it! BUT we have much in our lifestyle that we like, and would be loath to relinquish <u>unless</u> we could find a place that offered us more. And I guess that would be a physical situation much the same as this one which was directly involved in some work which gave us access to other people of like mind — preferably ones I could nominate — with whom one could engage in some 'growing' activities.

*

My work — whatever it actually is, and I struggle to get clear about this too — is very exciting to me these days. I seem to be having a lot of ideas that I enjoy throwing around and hammering out. Gradually, I'm realizing more time for reading and thinking, and I have some friends with whom I have many, very exciting conversations — we are trying to discipline these conversations, and bring some serious study into them and it is working — which in itself is very gratifying. I'm also still active in the Women's groups... in a kind of "catalyst" role. As an example of who come to these groups, a group I am active in consists of a very mixed lot: 6 American students 25 years old or under, 5 are single, one is married; 5 married mothers, age 29-32, who are all well-educated, intelligent and for the time being fairly actively involved and committed to their young children — but also to themselves as individuals and to a conscious relationship with their husbands; and 3 divorced mothers in their middle 30's — with children, who are very much struggling to make some sense out of their life. Everyone is somewhat interested in Anthroposophy but in very different degrees. We move around and around the theme of what does it really mean to be a woman today — as an experience but also from a spiritual point of view. Because of the age differences and the differences of life experience, there is always very lively, and sometimes very tense, discussion, but on the whole I think it's something everyone finds meaningful. I am certainly learning a lot — especially about the ways people react and interact in a mixed group situation. The other group I am involved in is very different—mostly young mothers with small children whose husbands are students. The group is on practical questions of nutrition, health, festivals, etc., but underlying the topics is the great need some of the women have to reach out of their loneliness and isolation—and <u>meet</u> others.

The playgroup we started here is so far very successful. Amazingly everyone is staying involved and participating — the kids almost always seem to be having a really good time... It's been so much easier than I'd anticipated... The kids even play with (**Waldorf**) dolls made by the local Women's Institute. We have quite a large number of children — 15–22 — and about 8–12 parents most weeks. I enjoy it all — even to my amazement the organization. Came as quite a shock to me, to realize that there are some things I can do better and with much less effort now at, nearly, 30, than I could 5 or 10 years ago. Came equally as a wonderful surprise to realize there may be more I can do better at 40, 50, 60 and so on. Very basic, but quite new to me, and very exciting. Realize I'm only just growing out of the idea that if you haven't done 'it' by the time you're 21, you never will.

*

At a recent group, everyone told how they experienced a real breaking off point at 21 — shedding whole parts of themselves. One walked out of a marriage — literally just walked out one day after waking up knowing it was finished. Another felt the peace of the end of a difficult adolescence but was rather on a pedestal and then experienced being knocked off — had to recognize selflessness. The confrontation of self-indulgence and reality — to do with birth of ego. All travelled in this period, with a great need to be 'free' of past ties — made breaks with old situations, loves — then moved into *very* different situations and people — i.e. people they would never have wanted to meet before — looked back on earlier years with a certain distance. Many expressed how they never thought of the importance of 21, but now they could see it was a special time — see the value of *perspective*!

*

After describing a women's group retreat day

It was a very good day — we couldn't really do everything

but not because we were careless — it really was too ambitions a plan — though we did a bit of everything.

We all do seem to want to go on — perhaps in some work/ karmic study/ anthroposophically deepening way. We seemed to share a sense that we must act more seriously within anthroposophy — prepare ourselves more adequately for what is to come. The way may be through a deeper study of our connections — of karma as such.

But also, we seem to share the feeling that as a *group* we have tasks — perhaps the conscious consolidation of the sort of community tasks we already do — and more.

∗

I haven't found it as easy as I thought I would to enter back into teaching. I think both of us were immediately so busy with settling in and with school work — we hardly had ½ hour to ourselves for about 8 weeks — that we were getting out of touch — with ourselves, with each other, with the essentials of life. I think you know what I mean. It seems as though I was behind before I began which is hard for me to deal with when starting something new.

∗

This was written by a participant returning home after one of the early public workshops — "Feminine and Masculine and the Challenge of Balance" — offered by the original Ariadne group.

I feel a real warmth — like some sort of real treasure, which I have to save in a very special place, where I can look at it and use a little bit of it in the future, when I discover again that my understanding of other people has not been as it should have been. I think that this weekend is a great help to become conscious of my own feminine qualities and maybe how to use them. I knew that the masculine part in myself was much stronger, but still it was a bit painful to discover that that part was so dominating. I hope that I can develop a bit of warmth with which I can help other people, not only 'me' but also other women.

✳

We were thinking and sharing about phases, especially the question of 21–28. If ideally one would be out experiencing the world openly, finding the self, what is the relationship of this wish — destiny? need? — to <u>being</u> responsible for a child/family — for a woman or man? We discussed the need to find balance, bring consciousness to decisions and their possible ramifications — one <u>can't</u> lead the more 'settled' life of the 30's in the 20's. Yet this 'having a child' is the <u>reality</u> your particular being must meet.

✳

People are calling me for private 'conversations' — I have a glimpse of a counseling possibility — and of the very great needs.

*

So now we have this land and this debt. So my fertile little mind begins to devise ways and means of earning a little money while I'm here at home with the children — something I can do in the house — breed fleas? — that won't be so engrossing or demanding that I can't bear to stop, or can't afford to. So, I began making cakes — all very purist — to sell in (a local) shop. It's not my <u>favorite</u> occupation, but it's something I <u>can</u> do, and even with the limited time available, it is a fairly reasonable financial prospect. One of the reasons I have less time than I might, is that I have begun a food co-op that requires quite a bit of paperwork and organization. I find to my amazement, I'm good at it — and quite enjoy it. If it was anything other than food, I couldn't raise the enthusiasm. There are enough people around, who are interested in obtaining organically grown grains, lentils, nuts, etc. to make it worthwhile… I've begun a playgroup, for the six children who are all born within a six-week period. It is so far — two months — very successful, and I enjoy it enormously. Of course, they are so tiny, they don't really play with each other, but <u>do</u> play round each other, and I love watching them. <u>And</u> I'm about to buy a loom. How can I be such a maniac as to imagine I'll ever have time to weave? But I <u>HAVE</u> to do something craft-creative. My soul absolutely cries out for color/texture/form. And I <u>will</u> make time, for that reason alone. I refuse to live another week without it!!!

✳

We are trying to move the school... for the beginning of the school year. An anthroposophist donated 20 acres of land to the school — it's good land for a school, a little far from (the city) but not <u>too</u> too far. We have to get some money to put <u>some</u> building on the site. Have been given $15,000 and possibly another $10,000 and with that can buy an old wooden hospital, move it there and start with that! All complex, but all we can afford. We're in the process of trying to get it all sorted out. It's wearying — all the energy one needs to coerce bureaucracy!

✳

Here is a letter sharing at length ideas for an article the writer was working on.

If women want to develop themselves, if mothers feel that they are more than only mothers, that they are also a person, is the only outcome to take a job in society? So many women with a profession feel that they can grow or develop in that profession, in that work. So if they become a mother, they feel the need to continue their work in society because they don't see the possibility to develop just by themselves, in a small circle with one or two little children, being at home all the time.

First, I had the feeling I had to give an answer to the

question: should women stay at home with their children or not? Now I know that it is impossible to give such an answer. It will be different for each woman, each child, each family. What I wanted to say in the article was that mothers need to recognize their own needs, the needs of their children, the needs of family life, and the needs of their husbands. Mothers have to meet each other and try to create together situations for each, which will be as positive as possible.

You can come together in women's groups and talk about womanhood. That is very important. Being a mother of small children I feel that I need first to talk about motherhood. What is this profession? What is this task? How can you discover your own development in this work? How can we prevent the isolation, and how can we create circumstances in which we can realize needs such as: study/ conscious exchange of experiences/ conscious growing and development/ knowhow about development of children/ etc.?

If a woman has a profession in society, she has colleagues with whom she consciously can develop her work. If you are a beginner, you can get supervision. You can work on problems you have with the relationship between yourself and your work... Women who become mothers, have a job in which they work very much with their soul. Some of them still can handle this intuitively, but most of them — as I — not. So I think that mothers have to work consciously on their soul life and they need others, other adults... But it seems still to be a realm about which one doesn't talk. I find myself time after time as a 'call in the desert.' Just no feedback, no answers. I find it hard to push myself in (social) situations to really ask attention for the value of the work I do. If we women cannot find a way in which these things can develop, I think more and more women will choose to work in society. More and more women will continue the job or profession, in which they are appreciated as a person of value — a lawyer, teacher, doctor or therapist is accepted in society as an interesting person. You can always find people with whom you can have good and interesting conversations about your work. You can experience yourself as a person in that kind of work.

And just in this time, this age, this century it is so important that children have parents around who give time/ love/warmth and understanding. But then parents — and at the moment mostly women — need help, need support of the surroundings to <u>do</u> this difficult job. They need help with ideas, motivation, and positive circumstances in which they can develop too... Otherwise, I think that the most clever, creative, active women will send their children to crèches and play-groups in order to continue their own important societal work.

(Some people) want to work with mothers, not so much with women. I want to work with mothers <u>as women</u>, not only as play-group leaders or handcraft people. A mother is a <u>worker</u> in the sense of a doer, she <u>does</u> things all the time: to do, to do, to do all day. But she has also a thinking and feeling pole. Her feeling and thinking parts also need to develop, need form and support, training. Doll-making is important but also what does a doll mean for <u>me</u>? How can I relate a doll to daily life, to social life? How can I share the phenomena 'doll' with my husband and other friends? This sounds mad and heavy, but I try to show that mothers need to find a way to communicate what they do with their surroundings. If they don't, they come into an isolated position for 10 or 20 years.

If women want to take care for this communication, they need space and time to work on it. This is a question of freedom. Can women make clear for themselves and for others that it is legitimate to ask this? How much motherly qualities do we really have? If you utter this question, many mothers will tell you that you shouldn't complain, that you should be humble, grateful and happy. This is for sure a matter of generations. My — our — generation wants to take seriously what is missing, lacking or not good in ourselves. The older generation tries to hide the mistakes and shows only the successes.

✳

Here is the same friend describing a mother's group that met over two years.

How much have we realized the aspect of our common <u>profession</u>, our <u>colleagueship</u>? How much have we stimulated each other by the fact that we all have worked on a <u>common</u>

aim: to help to develop future adults? You can feel so isolated in your own little house with your own little social group of 4 or 5 people. Being conscious about the solidarity with other mothers, other 'colleagues', it is perhaps possible to discover more objective sides of this profession instead of seeing how much it all is a muddle of subjectivities.

When a group of mothers do experience themselves as colleagues, like people who share the same profession, then it can be possible that you create possibilities to study, to plan, and to evaluate the work. It can be possible then that you feel again that you learn from the work, that you can develop yourself in that work. But I have experienced how difficult it is, because of the way in which we still do our work: all energy has gone when the evening starts. No one has taken time to prepare, etc. This becomes an endless circle. This circle has to be broken by women who have older children, so they have again some time to think!

The aspect of profession and colleagueship comes in because I miss so much these things in motherhood. When you have a job where you work with other people... you have your fixed moments of communication about the work, about aims, about the quality of the work, about possibilities to develop the work, etc.

As long as we were mothers in the sense of taking care of children, preparing things and content for them, it was quite easy. From the moment that we were together as adults, as persons who wanted to grow because of themselves, there became a gap. (In preparing for a festival) we did it for the children. There was no common content which was consciously shared by the adults... In such moments, I really miss the experience of sharing on my personal, adult level. I share in as much as I am a mother, working for the children. But I am more, too.

Again and again it seems so difficult to make space for this aspect of life. There is time to make decorations or to learn a song, but there is no time to read a lecture about festivals. There is time to bake cakes and to paint Christmas cards, but no time to speak as an adult with other mothers about the meaning of Christmas... In the mothers' group we also worked a bit on the question of learning to look consciously at our children. What do you really see, objectively? Observation exercises. This is a realm where you can develop your adult side. And at the same time, it is important for a better realization of your profession. (For example) we spoke about the three main qualities, which develop in the 3 times 7 years: thankfulness (0–7), beauty (7–14), truth (14–21). How can you bring such aims into practice? If you were a teacher you would have special weekend conferences or evening studies to get a grip on such important things. Now, being a mother 'the world' — and we too — think that you will know these things just naturally... Mothers' groups can grow into importance if women can accept or introduce the more common, the more objective side of their work, their capacities, their tasks. When they learn to translate their occupation onto a larger scale. To translate values out of family life into society, schools, work with their men, etc.

*

College begins tomorrow — I like this just-before anticipation. The names are there, the groups are made — but the real people have yet to come together. So many relationships which will become — but what, and how?

We had important faculty discussions. How can we best <u>practice</u> a real form of inner schooling together — so that the work is properly carried?

*

This friend had recently moved to a new country.

(My husband and I) are running a biography course in a few weeks together, and I am helping run a course for new mothers. I thought my contribution could be 'motherhood as a life crisis' and 'ambivalence!' We start in ten days and haven't discussed it yet, and I wonder what on earth I am doing, but I felt I had to say yes to something as I was, and still am, in great danger of resisting everything new.

*

1981 – 1982

In 1981, my family and I moved from England, to Detroit, Michigan, and I began teaching at The Waldorf Institute, an adult education center working with many of Rudolf Steiner's ideas, and in particular, training future Waldorf teachers. Four years later, the entire Institute moved to Spring Valley, New York and eventually was renamed Sunbridge College. The Ariadne work in England, which I left with my move back to the States, continued to develop, and I would hear about it from several different friends. I was also trying to bring some of this work alive in my teaching and in my new community. In these years, many of my friends and I were stepping more strongly into a variety of working situations: college teaching, Waldorf teaching, counseling, art therapy, care of people with special needs, etc.

Last weekend we had our Ariadne meetings — two after-noons in the end instead of a day. It was good. We held you with us strongly, and (a colleague) was able to read your letter…(which) meant so much to us all. The gap you have left in our lives is <u>enormous</u>, but at the same time you are always a part of us — that to me feels <u>very</u> real… When we looked at our individual years we all realized how overloaded our lives are . . . other part time work, health concerns, courses of study, moving house, etc. I feel our responsibility to our work and to each other and find it hard to make a decision. At the moment, we are trying to start with weekly meetings and will have our Ariadne Day on Saturday. The workshop is planned for November, and we talked a lot about the Adult Education Program on Family Life for the late Spring Term. It sounds good — I do hope we will be able to carry it through.

*

Ariadne will have a workshop in November on The Meaning of Feminine and Masculine in our Search for Wholeness — although we are still playing with the title. I hope we get the brochures out by the end of this week.

(The eventual title was: The Interweaving of Feminine and Masculine in our Lives)

*

We had a truly wonderful weekend… I could fill a whole letter telling you all about it! It just came at the right time for me, and I received many very helpful gifts from the lectures and the group work. (A friend) was at the weekend and after the first lecture she came up to me and asked me if I had been thinking of you — we both felt you there very strongly — the strange experience I had was that I could 'see' you <u>in</u> (the one giving the talk) as she spoke — I don't use the word 'see' in its usual sense! It was strange but comforting! We had five men on the course which I felt was a very good thing and I experienced absolutely no inhibiting effect — nor did anyone else, I know. (The speaker) lectured really well, and I think everyone who took part found it enlivening and thought-provoking.

✳

I was so aware of you during our workshop. All the time really — but suddenly and very strongly at the Sunday evaluation about 4:00. What were you doing then? — The Workshop was good. People were very positive. It was good to have more community people.

✳

My group (at the local college) is a wonderful group of people — very lively and strong and talented. We've been telling biographies. The exercise was to describe the environment you grew up in or have lived in for some length of time, and then either a wonder, or a significant meeting, or a significant decision you made in your life. Most people have done that and also managed to tell their whole life as well. And clearly, many people needed to say it and hear it from others and ask each other — "How did you come here?" I am always amazed at what people have had to cope with in their lives, and this time, especially, I have experienced a real awe and wonder for the strength and endurance of the human spirit — for that really shone through so many of their stories of crisis and conflict and great difficulties. I really feel it as a privilege to be able to work in these kinds of groups, and because of that I feel it as a tremendous responsibility to work in them consciously — knowing what we are doing and being able to carry them in such a way that they are fruitful for the students. We can enjoy them too, but they aren't primarily for us.

I've also joined the care group... (A new member) feels the College should try to find a counselor who they could recommend students to go to — because she feels — and I agree — that many students need real therapy, not just an ear to listen to them and kind and helpful words. I suggested the College might want to pay for me to have a training! And on first thought people seemed to think it might be a good idea. I didn't plan the suggestion, but I'm already far into imaginations of how it would work. Again this year, I've had talks with students where I felt I needed a training to really be able to help. Felt out of my depth. And I think this won't go away in my life, and it is a real part of the kind of work I feel is important. I'm planning to do the two-week counseling course at the Centre in March. But it would be wonderful to be able to take out a year and go into something in depth and get a <u>training</u> — my need for a definition I guess.

*

You know I carry this Ariadne work deeply, centrally. For me it is ever expanding. The work we have done, the finished product so to speak, is only the very surface — maybe it's a foundation but the mansion is yet to be built. I think you and (your husband) will carry it — whatever it/Ariadne is — further in your life studies program — your life centre. For me, the vision of future directions is many faceted and buzzing around in me but totally fuzzy and inarticulate. I don't think I can do it on my own. I need others to help formulate and incarnate it… I don't know. Maybe we all just have to take it as it lives in us into our various works — or is Ariadne something in itself, connected but also separate?

*

After meeting one of the main speakers at a conference to do with Karma and Reincarnation

We had a few brief conversations, and in one he made some joke about Ariadne and <u>your</u> interest in women's lib. I corrected him, told him you were my <u>colleague</u>!!, etc. but let the slight flippancy remain. So, I told him later I wanted to talk to him again, and I planned to inform him a bit about the deep seriousness of Ariadne, but we never had that conversation. He was too busy, and I was too shy to remind him that I wanted to talk with him. So I'm sorry about that, because I felt he hadn't a clue about Ariadne and as many people — especially men — do at first, was trying to laugh it off. But maybe it doesn't matter.

＊

I'm enjoying stretching myself into an area I haven't really entered. There is so much I want to know… I'd like to withdraw and become a monk — again! I want to especially learn the names of plants and trees. And learn to <u>know</u> the stars.

＊

I have decided to wait on the counseling training. I think it won't go away. It has emerged very strongly out of this year, and I do think in some ways it is a thread towards my future. But maybe because it does seem so real, I am not frantic to do it now. I don't think I'm ready to pull out of home, and (work commitments), and I do feel if it's real there will be time — it will grow and emerge. Without a training I will or can anyway grow towards it and take it up more fully or professionally later. I fluctuate between feeling time is getting on — to feeling there is so much time, or will be when I know exactly what I want to do.

＊

Doing the group has brought up so much in me. Especially how much I enjoy working with you, how much the work for me has lived between us, how the true creativity for me came from the sharing and developing and enthusing, expanding and forming of the ideas one or the other of us had. I know and hope that that is not over. That it will find new ways. But also in many ways, physical and practical, it can't happen now. I know I can, and do, call on all that has been nurtured and opened in me from our relationship. But it is lonely and not nearly so much fun. It calls on a new strength, a kind of iron will which I feel I can have, do have, sometimes — and the love I feel for you has helped to forge that sword — but maybe because of all that such a transition means, doing this group now has flooded me with questions. I am really doing Ariadne work. But what is Ariadne work? I realize how bound up it is with my heart, which is bound up with you and our (women's) group. It lived so much for me in between our relationships. That's not to say it's not real work — it is, I guess it was always work, and objective, etc, but it came out of my love. So now the question of what it is haunts me.

The group goes really very well, yet I come home every day plagued with doubts which seem to have nothing to do with the group. People can — and do, don't they? — talk about relationships, sex — and those are their real questions — all the time. So what's so different about providing a space for a somewhat more formed discussion? People seem to want it, but what are we really doing? One thing I've realized very strongly this time is how <u>very, very</u> clear we have to be. I have watched with amazement how I can say something and five minutes later hear it back to front, upside down. Not their fault I think, but mine. Having such direct feedback does make me wonder how people have taken things out of our workshops. Except maybe clarity and objectivity are easier to achieve with lectures than in informal talks in the round, in small groups. And I think our work has been protected. But especially because these questions are so close to us all and can be quickly perverted, we must be very careful how we speak.

Later in the letter that went on for many days

My group was excellent, in spite of my many doubts and questions. I think some people were really helped, especially — as always — by listening to each other, gaining some sense of what other people's lives and hopes and struggles are.

※

There are staff workdays Tuesday-Friday. I've been asked to lead a discussion group — the theme is Work — on the evening lectures. I said "sure," and since I have been terrified. I was honored at first, now I just see it as presumptuous… Well, maybe it's pedagogical. Maybe it just means we have to take ourselves more seriously and get on with the work.

※

I realize that for me feminine and masculine is only an aspect — an important one — of what I feel my work is about. But what is it? What is my work?… Truly I think it may be awakening individuals to their creative origins and possible tasks — to their humanity — in many different ways. But feeling rather a dull stone myself at times, who am I to presume to do that? But I guess most of the time we see so little of who we are, what we are capable of. You held a picture for me of who I was or could be, and I could trust you, and for that there are no ways to tell you thank you. It's not even on that level somehow. But for me it was/is a gift — and how can I be crying here with laughing children, splashing water and sunshine? Anyway what I was thinking is how in those moments when we have to — a child hurt, giving a lecture, carrying a group — we can bring into us the full strength and courage and shining-ness of our ego, then we are so much larger and more capable than we feel we are in day to day fumblings. I guess we need to work to bring that force, that presence into life and to encourage its expression in others more often. But I'm going round the real question that keeps coming up — what is my task? What is Ariadne? What do I have to give?

*

Is Ariadne a developing impulse? How can it develop? Where is its future? This child that we brought to birth, how do we help it grow, how should it grow? What is its destiny and purpose?... I was walking blindly through (a nearby town), worrying until I suddenly realized it was useless to worry. I'll do what I can. We'll do what we can, and that's all. But when it comes to it, I realize I give it a lot of space, and I feel it is important not to let it go. Many people, not just in my group at the Summer School, were very interested and excited about our work, want to come to workshops, have taken out subscriptions for the newsletter. There are questions coming towards us.

＊

I must tell you how truly wonderful the weekend... was. Getting on the train I felt almost sick with anxiety, but after 5 minutes I realized it was going to be an adventure and it was! I loved getting away, seeing and hearing what was happening in Anthroposophy in the North, making new connections, meeting new people. I loved working with (a colleague) and between us I felt Ariadne, whoever she is, was living, breathing freely again for a moment, and warming the people present... My lecture was a surprise to me in that it was wonderful to give and wonderfully received. There was a kind of grace given so that it was also what it was trying to say. I can only say that because it has been so long since I felt the <u>depth</u> in between what I have tried to say and the listening in the room, and I felt a lightness afterwards. It was research not wisdom, simple and basic and questioning, and people seemed glad for that — thank goodness. And because it wasn't all said, there was much discussion in groups in the day... It was mainly about being <u>in</u> time, in the present, and thinking within things, open to what meets us. About the fall from rhythm and why, and about ways to begin to work consciously with building an inner rhythm and outer rhythms again. About overcoming of stress and anxiety, about the rhythms of the creative process. In a way, it's a beginning of that work we were going to do for a workshop once upon a time. I feel there is a sort of seed within me now around which and out of which things might grow. A beginning.

We had a very informal meeting with about 12 people who were interested to know what Ariadne was and did... I spoke of the history of Ariadne and areas of research. (A colleague) filled in what I left out — all very briefly. But it sparked such a fiery conversation with some people furiously denying there was a question — "There is no sex in the spiritual world!" — and in the next breath attacking each other for being typically male or female. However, most people were truly interested, understanding and wanting to explore calmly! By the end of the 1½ hour it was clear that there definitely was a <u>question</u> and people thought perhaps there should be a weekend... (My colleague) was so strong and clear about what Ariadne is — "Rudolf Steiner encouraged us to investigate the physical world... there are no crystals in the spiritual world, but should we not investigate crystals? Just because we are not male or female in the spiritual world does not mean we should not investigate the polarity as we meet it on earth. Ariadne is doing real and new spiritual research."

*

Many people over the years have come to value our work and its quality, people who don't want to be busy with it themselves, but have seen its importance and the responsibility and depth with which we approach it. I don't think we've been strident, or fanatic, or divisive. We've <u>tried to develop and nurture</u> in ourselves what we talk about.

*

I have decided not to be blown about by the struggles of my philosophers this year (**study group working with Rudolf Steiner's** *Philosophy of Freedom*) and so far, I'm really enjoying it and feel finally more confident. I love the group I'm working with and although there have been struggles — between the intellectual, stick-to-the-book people and the experience people — I feel we are strongly working. I do <u>love</u> the book so much; the activity it demands of me, the warmth it fills me with through the working. Each year I begin the journey new, yet each year something grows stronger in me, something that does stay with me. The chance to work with the book in this way gives me so much more than I can give. I'm sure of that.

*

I might take on the *Review* (**a Steiner-related literary magazine**) theme for next autumn. Maybe something of a continuation of the Man/Woman issue, but — Questions of Freedom or something like it. Bringing in abortion and homosexuality, both of which we've had many requests and letters for and about. Also the concept of the free spirit. It's in seed form still. But I'll let you know because I may want you to write.

1983 – 1987

I should take the opportunity to get on with my lecture planning. Why does it still take so much of me — so much energy… I guess there has been some progress. It took me over 3 months to prepare the first one. If I meet my deadline, I'll finish 5 in a week — but I know most of it already, so why the sweat, the total involvement, the terror, the perpetual trips to the bathroom already? What's it for?

Ariadne is such a big question to me. Doing these lectures and the group too, I realize one of our failings was training—no training. We trained each other — all of us together, and you and I particularly in the work we did for that first seminar. — I am still astounded at how much anthroposophy I read and understood in such a short space of time. Some things I understood better then than now. But some people who have worked with us afterwards have not had the <u>foundation</u> to move from... What do you think about training?... Should I offer a training group for people wanting to do the work? I can hardly imagine it.

*

The morning course lectures seem so far away now, and they were such an effort for me, but because the students were so receptive and interested, I did also enjoy them... I introduced the theme by exploring the women's movement — positive and negative, society today, levels of polarity, division of the sexes. Also, in the first morning I talked about the work of Ariadne and told the myth. Then the historical development... Then why am I a woman/man, relationships, conception of life — family life, rhythm, abortion, etc — ending with New Isis.[1]

---

1   This mention of the New Isis refers to a modern myth told by Rudolf Steiner in which not the ancient Egyptian Goddess Isis is meant but rather the Isis of a New Age. First appearing as a statue, to most people this New Isis is invisible. She is veiled and she is asleep, but with an inscription above her head which reads: "I am the Human Being. I am the Past, the Present, and the Future. Every mortal should lift my veil." Eventually she bears an offspring whose father is unknown but certainly is not the powerful visitor who assumes that he is. Through the power of the modern world the offspring is broken into fourteen pieces, then put together by

It is clear that the questions we have worked with are still important, still being asked, maybe in a slightly different way. I think more men are asking why they are men now, and fewer women — but still I find many women and men who cannot relate to that question. They were very stimulated by the lecture, but when we took that question in my group, people found it difficult to answer personally.

We are in quite a panic over the family life evenings! (One colleague) is unable to give the talk on Divorce and Single Parents. Two others will be out of town. (Another) will give the first evening — an introduction, and What is Family Life? (A different colleague) will do Extended Families — so (two others) and I are left with Relationships and Marriage — Help! — Parenthood as a Path of Development, and

---

the visitor who is gifted in "scientific profundity." He then clones this re-created being into fourteen identical apparent offspring that obey only mechanical laws, and he gives each one his countenance. As the New Isis grows in spiritual vision through the help of nature beings, she is able to receive her offspring again in its true form. This strange and prescient story goes on with further descriptions that speak to our contemporary realities and the challenges we face to be awake in these times. For more on this modern myth, see Chapter 10 of my book, *Why on Earth? Biography and the Practice of Human Becoming*, Steiner Books, 2013; R. Steiner, *Ancient Myths and The New Isis Mysteries*, SteinerBooks, 2018; or R. Steiner, *Isis, Mary, Sophia: Her Mission and Ours*, Steiner Books, 2003.

aforesaid Divorce! We're not quite sure how it's to be parceled out! We were going to share the second one, but now (some) feel each of us should do an evening — or at least a ½ hour talk! (The hostess's husband) came strolling in to our last meeting, and we jokingly asked him if he'd give one of the talks. He said calmly, "I <u>could</u> but I won't." <u>We</u> said "We <u>can't</u> but we will!!" We fell about laughing, as it seemed such a typical male, female situation!

✳

The family life evenings have on the whole been going well. My impression for the first couple of weeks was — why had we waited so long! We really seem to be providing a space for much needed exchange and support on real and vital questions. We have 3 groups of about 11 each... The first evening I spoke — about 45 minutes — about family life in general today — some difficulties and possibilities. I looked at the Women's Movement, roles changing, difficulties in relationships, and at rhythm and reverence for the small, etc. The next Monday I also spoke about relationships, primarily, (then a colleague) spoke on divorce and single parenthood.

✳

Last weekend I helped with the Centre biography workshop — first time ever and I was very glad for the experience. How was your workshop? That's something else I'd like to talk with you about. I have so many fresh questions and ideas about biography work, which I feel is <u>so important</u> and also something I want to do and develop — somehow, sometime, somewhere... It seems to me the biography work is, among other things, a <u>method</u> for what Steiner speaks of in the 14th chapter of *The Philosophy of Freedom* — about taking into ourselves the concept of the other, developing interest in the other, listening in to their true being. I felt like a huge ear over those 3½ days, an ear learning how to hear the inner song or story written underneath the external script.

Can you train someone to work with Ariadne? What would such a training be comprised of — *Philosophy of Freedom*? *Knowledge of Higher Worlds*? Male/Female questions? Social Development training? Group work? Mythology? Public Speaking? It seems to me that people that I consider to be carrying Ariadne have a deep connection to Anthroposophy and in their own individual way can speak out of that, can listen into an imaginative realm within and without, have a sort of intellectual integrity — I don't mean intellectuals — do I mean standard?

Is Ariadne a personal, karmic thing between certain individuals, or is it a wider objective work that you can train people for? — I guess both could be true! This is another day-long discussion. Are you making a list of things we must talk about?... Who is Ariadne?

✳

(An older woman) wrote a curt note asking me to cancel her subscription to the Ariadne Newsletter because Rudolf Steiner said politics should be eliminated from the Anthroposophical Society, and anyway she doesn't support our politics. I wrote a good response back saying I was sorry, and sorry she didn't write an article about her views. But also saying Ariadne was not a Society journal — that anyway opinions expressed were those of the writers not the editors and a bit about what I thought Steiner meant by his statement about politics and the Society. Certainly not that we shouldn't try to understand the situations, dilemmas of today out of the perspective offered by Anthroposophy... Otherwise though, I have had only positive responses to the last newsletter — could you ask maybe two people, at least one man — both maybe mid-30's or so — how the 'will' has influenced their lives. Ask them to write a short account of its influence, positive and/or negative — a personal account.

✳

There are so many more single parents (at the college). Many more women than men and a number of queries that have drifted my way about Ariadne. In some ways I think Ariadne work becomes <u>ever</u> more important.

✳

I do think we should write something — something new, that would bring together and make visible, in a clear and <u>simple</u> way, the work done, the thoughts developed, the questions asked, the directions explored. I think it might help even to find the next step in this Ariadne work. I know the steps grow invisibly one after another. I know the work <u>is</u> ongoing if someone, some people are willing to go on, but maybe particularly for us it would help us sort out the past from the present and future.

＊

(A male colleague) asked me if I would do a group with him on "Who is Anthroposophia?"… Of course, I couldn't refuse such a challenge… The main plan is that <u>he will be respon-sible</u> for the first half, and I will <u>just participate</u>. Then when he goes away I'll carry it. The first part will try to look at the being of Anthroposophia — Sophia — Isis — The biog-raphy of Anthroposophy. Then I'll probably take it more into questions of feminine and masculine — the qualities, tasks and their balance and transformation. I really haven't thought much and am worried about doing <u>too much</u>… I'm looking forward to working with him because I think we come to many similar concerns from quite different places and I think working together could be fruitful — especially and mainly for me.

＊

Out of the lectures, a couple of weekly groups grew, which were nice but a bit loose — one for parents, which was very supportive, I think, and we talked about adolescence, sex education, single parenthood, the first months after birth, single parenthood when you are the absent parent, and guilt.

✳

Along with the groups, I got involved in more 'counseling' situations than ever before — more ongoing situations with students and a couple of community people — even one married couple who I resisted for a year and then finally felt I could try. So lots of new questions have come up, and I feel very inexperienced. I've found that I feel very uncomfortable with the professional counselor status and with the money side of it. I've found although I work very intuitively, that is no longer enough. I realized that in the last biography workshop, too. It went well, and so far so does the counseling, but I feel more and more I'm skating on thin ice. I need more form, more depth in understanding of what I'm doing. I guess I'm still drawing on 'old forces' and too lazy to create new ones. Well, it's not just laziness, I feel at a loss to know how, partly. I'd love to have a working group on biography and counseling, but it never happens — and I never make it happen... So how do we educate ourselves to what we — I anyway — have taken on without enough preparation?

I Give You My Word

*

Well, the Newsletter, I think, is finally and utterly over! But I've promised myself that I would — and you would!? — get together one last good issue — which would include a picture of Ariadne (activities) in England, America, Holland, and, I heard today, New Zealand — a letter from someone who has just started a group, research and consciousness raising, working with old newsletter material and wants to call it Ariadne — asks if they can, as they feel they are 'picking up the thread' there! Also, a farewell speech, address, from us — would you like to write it? We already have the article on Rosa Mayreder, an article on (our colleague's) work with Peace and Women's questions, maybe a lecture on conception and birth by Thomas Weihs to reprint, maybe an article on the latest developments in fertilization and the Warnock Committee report. What else? Can you think of something — or solicit something? Maybe I can also get a report of the Emerson Peace Conference. People continue to subscribe and say how important the newsletter is to them — so I think we owe it to them and to ourselves to have a grand finale!

*

I can't remember if I wrote you about my questions about counseling. I was busy with many different 'helping conversations' last year, several ongoing ones, one where I was actually paid. Plus the counseling course at the Center, and I ended up with many vague questions about counseling — about what I was doing, if I knew what I was doing, if I had the capacity, did I really want to counsel, did I want to earn money from it?... Professional training of any kind still seems years away. And when the possibility is there, of time to train, there are many things I'd like to do — maybe a more thorough counseling training, but maybe painting or voice, or drama and speech. Something to balance my terrible one-sidedness. All and any such things would mean facing myself in a rather painful way, but the release and development would be worth it.

*

I've been enjoying the students this year very much — in groups and in individual conversations. I even enjoyed giving my morning course. Next term (a colleague) and I may do a parenting group together — or, if people are interested, I thought I'd like to do a group on biography using Lievegoed's book (*Phases*) as a basis but looking at male and female development and questions through a study of phases. A group of us who do biography workshops are also trying to take that further.

*

I do wonder how it would be to be back in that scholarly world. I'm still working through the Natura book you sent me, and I find it interesting and helpful, but very slow because it is <u>so</u> dry and scholarly. It's a burning question for me, a life question, and a question relevant to our times — the relationship to Isis, Sophia, Mary, or Natura — and yet someone can write such a book without any hint of personal interest, questions, or even the questions of others today. Just holding a microscope on a particular theme in history, not for it's meaning but for itself. I do admire it, but I couldn't do it — I'm not sure I ever could.

✳

Do you have or hear much response from people about *Lifeways*? (*Lifeways: Working with Family Questions*, Ed. Gudrun Davy & Bons Voors, Hawthorn Press, 1983). I liked being able to refer to it — especially your chapter — in my lectures last year. It was good to be able to point people to some relevant reading on relationships. On and off I get wonderful, encouraging and warming letters from people I don't know, who thank me for my chapter... Truthfully, I feel <u>very</u> detached from 'my' chapter — and I don't really feel very personal about it at all. I just think it's good to have the book around.

✳

I have been asked to talk in October for the National Childbirth Trust. <u>INFO 3</u> has asked me to write on masculine and feminine, I get letters regularly asking about

Ariadne, asking for help. People ask me still and contact me about homosexuality, about contraception. About the Feminine and Peace — that is a growing work of mine, and also connected with the theme of the need to find the New Isis <u>today</u>... I want to offer morning groups in the village too, on masculine/feminine and *Lifeways*, but I can't imagine when. I want to help develop a parents' course at (the college) too. I want to work with all this — am glad for the questions, requests, yet feel like I'm forever plodding on alone.

Do I have to continue to ask myself what should I be doing? Am I a lost soul with no direction, able to step into any direction but having none?... Isn't it pathetic to be 42 and at such a loss? I wish I could be clearer. Sometimes I look at my life and see failure and only that — family, work, relationships, everything. And of course (my teenager) tells me that constantly. Mostly I think that's not entirely true ... but what do I really have to give?

CHAPTER 6

Letters as a Living Link

One theme that recurs again and again in the letters is the importance of the actual words that my friends and I were writing and receiving. There is the obvious, if painful, recognition that given the many miles between us, letters were necessary to support each other's continuing development, and also to deepen the friendship itself. Sometimes there is an effort to address questions or comments that must have been aired in my letters — to carry on and deepen the conversation.

Some writers explore the nature of friendship, and specifically of our particular relationship. Writing letters allowed us to articulate how important we were to each other. While it might seem that the focus in some of these excerpts is on me, I hope readers will understand that I share them knowing that they are not only about me. They express how important friends are in our developing lives. There are often apologies for the inadequacy of words to truly say what is in the writer's heart, but also deeply felt expressions of gratitude for the life-giving link that the letters provide.

1973 – 1975

We had two letters from you… so good to get them both… I had so many things I wanted to say to you as I read — and the unexpected bonus of two instead of one was great for anyone as greedy as I am. I read them both five times in ½ an hour — and then went up to look for more — just in case! I laughed at myself all the way up to the mailboxes.

As for your question about how we can best help our relationship to grow — it <u>is</u> difficult, when the only tangible form of communication one has, is letters — but then, <u>whenever</u> I read a letter from someone I am really close to, it is so <u>with</u> me and I with it, in a real communion, that I feel it must travel. And I usually know when the letter is coming. I also think, to enter, as much as possible, into whatever each other of us is doing — both in thought and reading and even meditation — that must be positive.

＊

Do you find you can carry around an unwritten letter in your head and somehow be lulled into thinking it got written and mailed and almost be waiting for an answer? Well it's clear that that's the kind I've been writing you lately — and I'm sorry. Still, you are as always very actively in my thoughts.

I just spent too much of this evening cleaning my desk. Of course I have tons of other things I should, and want, in an inactive sort of way, to do — admittedly most of what I would have needed in order to do any of the things — like your letter — was hidden in the mountain of disarray of my desk. Still, I find that cleaning my desk is less of an activity than a mental state. Do you know what I mean?

*

I couldn't believe that 18-page letter! It was like being given a good book.

*

Why don't you develop your telepathic faculties and send me some 'vibes' — not that I would know how to pick them up.

*

This is impoverished and hasty in case I don't get time to write more. I want to go on and on, especially to reply to things in your last letter, but I want to get something down and away to you, now, while I've got 10 minutes, and I daren't start more than I <u>know</u> I can finish... This thing, though, of NEVER having time — I mean — it <u>must</u> get better, surely — or does it get worse? I have had this letter in my head to you since I got yours — at least a week ago, and I swear, I have not had <u>one</u> minute to write to you — not even this piddling air letter's worth. Do you know how frustrating that can be? Everything conspires against it.

✳

Your letters are not too heavy — I wouldn't want you to censure what's happening to you. I just want to stay in contact with how you are and what you are doing and thinking — whatever that is.

✳

Your last letter was so good to get — so much in it I want to talk to you about. That thing about liking and disliking being the greatest danger to real meeting is true, I'm sure — certainly true for me. But what the difference is, in friendship, for me, is that I <u>love</u>, when I do, and that is the greatest possibility for real meeting, I think. If you can truly love, — or approach it, or be conscious of what that is — then it is the way that you can work to help each other — that you can <u>want</u> to, and be to a certain extent selfless in this without 'realizing' necessarily that that is what you are doing.

*

I need more time between us before I can really talk to you about our friendship and what it is to me. I realize, as I read your letters, that already part of me lives in the future of our relationship, even though I know we don't know what or when that future is or will be. I am still much too close to the physical reality of you to be really able to look back much — in a way, I guess that's partly why I look forward. I miss you as much as I knew I would, and with an ever-pres-entness that foreknowledge does nothing to diminish. I think the only way I am able to <u>believe</u> so much in 'the future,' is because I feel we have so much further to go with each other — I really feel we have just begun and somehow this, for me, ties into the question you have about "whether we could know each other so well, and with such intensity because... we had only this year." Undoubtedly there was a 'temporal consciousness,' but I don't really think <u>this stage</u> of our relationship would have been — could have been?? — any different — even if we had had the possibility of 50 years in front of us. It was as intense, and as meaningful and as <u>real</u> as it <u>was</u>, and not, I think, because it had to be fitted into a particular space of time. I think certain exter-nal events aided and abetted its growth — just as others hindered... I think that whatever we are to each other in the future, it will probably never be able to be as easy and as joyful as this year was — but then, maybe that's <u>why</u> this year was what it was? I, too, feel grateful and so much more

— I will write to you more of that when I am a little further away from the first acute missingness that I now feel.

*

1976 – 1978

Mutual friends were coming to visit this writer.

We had a card from them last week saying they'd be (coming in July), and I immediately had the most incredible rush of emotion. Mostly a longing to see them, a longing to have that little contact with you, a longing to experience a little of our past, a longing to see someone familiar — and I mean that in a slightly broader sense than the physical, I think. Anyways, in thinking later about this — very intense — reaction, I realized this: that if someone had asked me, "Are you lonely?" I'd have said "No, of course not" quite definitely — you know me… and I'd have believed I was speaking the truth. But I realized that I probably am, much more than I can even admit to myself, in a soul-life way, much, much more than in a day-to-day communication way, though that exists too, as there is no one around here to talk to, let alone really talk to, though I must admit it's only the latter I miss. It's not that we are so isolated even, for by (local) standards we aren't at all; the next house isn't so far away — but I swear, I have no idea if anyone lives there — I've never seen any sign of activity when I've been hanging

the flags of my industry — nappies — on the washing line...
I guess I do feel lonely. I love (my husband) coming home,
and I find great solace in my head and the letters I write
there, finding more time to do that than to write them anywhere else. And I don't think I even <u>mind</u> the loneliness, so
this is in no sense a complaint, merely a making conscious
of something I really had not noticed.

I have a rare illicit 20 minutes before (my husband) comes
home for lunch when there's nothing I absolutely cannot
ignore... It feels so good to sit here with you in my heart
and to just ramble on. Stuff discipline.

Somehow correspondence poses a problem for me that it
never used to... Now there's a funny balance that has to be
met; it doesn't make sense to write just about events that
occur in our lives nor to write just about what we're thinking about: writing about how those two interpenetrate is
what I'd like to do, carefully, but that's difficult and I always
wait for the day — when? — when I'll have the time at
once, to sit and think and write a whole coherent letter.
That time doesn't seem to come.

Here is an example of the beginning and ending of a 10-page letter — the body of which was full of descriptions of work on the farm, the baby, her pregnancy, the politics of the local farming community, the beauty of the garden, etc.

I have raced through everything to be able to spend a few pages with you, at least... I should begin this, not with the feeling of how much will I write before (the baby) gets pissed off and demands I take some notice of her, but just write, and *calmly*. And I will, or try to...

... I am so dissatisfied with this letter I can hardly bear to send it — but daren't not send it for fear of how long it will be before I write the next one! I refuse to let it be long, and get depressed when I realize that anyway it will be longer than I would like.

✳

It is the 29th of December, and I <u>still</u> haven't had a single worthwhile contraction. I am in that limbo that always comes when you've said goodbye to one phase — in this case nine months of pregnancy — but haven't yet begun on the next — raising the child — and I am SHATTERED that I haven't yet managed to complete a decent letter to you. I guess that's one good thing about the baby not choosing it's time yet — at least I <u>may</u> get one written now if my mother can manage to keep sweet (older child) occupied for the next 10 hours or so. Though I must say, beginning defeats me — there is <u>so</u> much. I wonder if I should just parcel up all the unfinished beginnings I've begun over the last three months. Except I can't bear the chaos and disorder they reveal.

5 pages later

Now it's next morning — I've got to go shopping and would love to post this — so that you know we're still alive, if nothing else. But I wanted to <u>really</u> write to you, and this is hardly that! The constant dilemma — do I (mail) what is finished so that at least that's there, or do I keep it, waiting for time and space to write the great thoughts I constantly think to you? I guess I'll post this and this other fragment I found yesterday when I was looking for paper to write to you on.

※

I have been busy in my mind a lot with you. I have had many 'talks' with you. It has been strange for me to miss the women's group, to miss a place where I could exchange thoughts and feelings...

Many times I wanted to write you about our situation, but then it was so complicated and also so black that I stopped. It's strange to write somebody about problems. I could feel the need to express myself to you, but at the same time I was conscious that I then only would give a 'black picture,' and I didn't want to give only such a one-sided picture. I had to write other things, too, but I couldn't.

✳

After describing multiple activities and responsibilities

Maybe you'll understand why you've heard so little from us, though you <u>must</u> get my thoughts. Surely. They are so frequent and so strong; I often wonder if Rudolf Steiner would have considered you, my dearest, an appropriate subject for meditation. Letter writing, which I enjoy and <u>need</u> to do — even if only because I <u>need</u> letters to arrive — and which is a constant priority in my life, has just been something I haven't done for the last 3/4 months. When the children are awake, I'm with them — and they carefully arrange to stagger their sleeping most of the time — and when they are asleep, I'm baking, or doing co-op sums, or cleaning, or washing nappies, or, or, or, or, or.

✳

I have really realized more and more these last few weeks how important the 'old group' was for me. Somehow, whatever else went on during the week, there was that time when I was together with friends. It has also hit me — the depth of our work together. Not only caring and sharing but really taking one another's growth seriously and always supporting in whatever ways were possible. I miss that and haven't found it here yet.

✳

In terms of your questions… It raises questions for me about being an outsider or feeling myself to be one — which is something I have to look at. I know that sometimes I find myself envious of your friendships, as I found it difficult to make connections at Emerson in an easy way. I also always felt a need to bring something to consciousness in my relationship with you, but I was never sure exactly what it was. I rehearsed several conversations with you, but I never got close enough to what I wanted to say to actually talk with you. Sometimes I find my phlegmatic, melancholic side more than I can cope with. All this is to say I feel on some level we have something to carry further, but I don't know what. I hope this makes sense.

✳

I am determined you shall have a birthday letter. The usual paralysis of being unwilling to write less than a minute by minute description of my life in the last six months prevails, and I'm still waiting, as I've waited these past two years for that stretch of uninterrupted time in which <u>really</u> to write to you… Now both *kinders* are *ins Bett*, and long may they stay there; your letter will be as long as they do! It's so long since I've written more than a shopping list, I have already got cramp!

I must try shorter letters (**this particular one is 12 large pages**), more often, but you've heard that before, too.

I long for a letter from you, but — amazingly — don't hate you when there aren't any. Just wish I could see you. We've been here two years now… I'm sorry this is such a scramble — I would love it to be legible, coherent and full of wisdom, but you'll just have to settle for this hodge-podge instead.

✳

Here is another example of a long protracted letter:

I'm lying in bed. So either I'll fall asleep, or this will be so illegible, I won't send it. An exercise in pointlessness one way or another, my letters seem to be these days.

(two pages of vivid details about the children)

I wrote all that about three weeks ago and haven't touched it since. I'm ashamed of how <u>complaining</u> it is (**though it wasn't**). I'm sorry for having indulged myself to that extent — I must have been feeling low!… I cannot remember when last I wrote to you, or what I've told you. I don't want to get bogged down in detail about our life here, though if I start to describe any of it, I undoubtedly will. The house we live in is really very satisfactory — we realize more and more how lucky we have been. (A) It's rather a nice old house — especially now that we've patched the holes in the walls and put glass in the windows, etc. — and (B) It doesn't cost us anything in rent, for we milk 60 Friesian cows every alternate weekend instead. Which is only about twelve hours work a fortnight, so it's a pretty good deal. There is <u>lots</u> of room for the children to play — i.e. fenced, mown — snake free — yard — and it's not too close to the road. `

(two more pages of lively descriptions of recent happenings)

And so that attempt ended too and now it's about six weeks later and I'm back in bed, falling asleep as I write. I cannot cope with how fast time is going — it is literally evaporating before my conscious eyes, and I get to feel quite desperate at times. Must be old age creeping upon me. (My husband) turned 36 and was depressed for days — he really identifies 40 with his mother — who is seventy or so, but he's forgotten that! — and can't quite cope with the thought of joining the ranks of the aged. I'm still fairly immune to the progress of time in relation to my life — I think! — but I must say, I am depressed by how fast each day zips off into the past.

(Yet another gap and then two more pages of descriptions of the children)

Whatever happens, I'll put this in an envelope tonight and post it off to you — it's such a hodge-podge of fragments, I can't stand it hanging around any longer.

✳

Have had several dreams about you over the past month — always had to do with meeting you in a positive way. Maybe I felt that we had in fact met and letters were no longer necessary???

✳

After an interruption after 5 initial pages

I stopped there and now it's after (our recent) phone call! I have always known a life of crime is not for me — I couldn't say so, at the time, but that phone call 'was arranged' by an employee of (the phone company) — and <u>was</u> supposedly foolproof. I was offered the chance and after a fair amount of moral to-ing and fro-ing I decided I'd do it. I enjoyed it — but not without suffering! Then, afterwards, the person who arranged it told me that if it is ever queried, you'll have to say it was a hoax call, from someone you don't know! I said, I thought you said it was foolproof! He said they'd had an unexpected supervisor check that night and he'd had to make out a receipt for that call. I'm terribly sorry — to implicate you as well! I don't know if I'm sorry I made the call — I am and I'm not, I guess. I'm not good material for cheating anyone any more. But I am sorry that you may eventually get a query about it. I really don't know what to do about that. Well, there's not much I can do now, except sit with crossed fingers and hope it doesn't happen. I'm not sure of the ins and outs of the whole thing — it's typical of my cowardice that I didn't ask. I said, "Don't you think it lasted a bit long to be able to be explained away as a hoax?' This guy said, "All mad hoaxers are big talkers!"

＊

1980 – 1981

Quoted in a letter:

Oath of Friendship — anonymous, China, 1ˢᵗ century BC

Shang ya!
I want to be your friend
For ever and ever without break or decay.
When the hills are all flat
And the rivers are all dry,
When it lightens and thunders in winter,
When it rains and snows in summer,
When Heaven and Earth mingle —
Not till then will I part from you.

＊

I speak of our leaving — consider the practicalities — and yet inwardly I wonder if I have taken it in — the enormity of the move... the changes it will mean for all of us. I cannot think of really leaving. I don't know how I will live without my friends. They are so much a part of my existence — of my thinking, feeling, doing. Now I just have a lump in my throat.

*

About Detroit... I appreciate your longings and fears, and ironic awarenesses. It almost seems too much to ask a mere human being to make such destiny decisions, doesn't it? Just think, we spend our whole childhood longing to make decisions of our own, only to resent them, often, when we have to, as adults... Of course, I can say so little — for myself, I find it hard to imagine living amongst such cityness, but that's undoubtedly very tied up with the children being so little. And there are always havens in suburbia, leafy and pleasant and less noisy — money usually secures them — will you have enough? — or will you be like us, and find a solution without money?... I eagerly await your decision.

*

It's a full-stretched time — sometimes I have felt like snapping and yesterday was very depressed. Being down/tired — I let all the sadness in me have a foothold — I felt I could cry for hours. But what good would it do? So I hold on.

*

Please don't worry about answering letters — it mustn't be a chore or a weight on your conscience. I just love writing letters — so I'll just continue, as long as I don't get bogged down doing lots of silly endless jobs, as before!

✳

At the end of a 31-page letter

I think reading all this requires flexibility, a keen eye and patience. I hope it hasn't been too hard going.

✳

I can't possibly be beginning this letter to you — surrounded as I am by unmade beds, unclothed children, unfolded nappies, unwashed dishes, un-hung-out clothes, un-lit fires and so on. But I am. Before I began, I <u>did</u> think — it is perfectly ridiculous to start <u>anything</u> else at the moment when you are already sewing trousers for the kids for winter, shirt for (my husband), knitting hats, making tomato sauce — in 24 lb. batches — YUCK! — have three different weaving projects underway and a sizeable dying project 1/3 complete; when you drive (the eldest child) to and from school for 1½ hours, three days a week and do cleaning job in nearby town one morning a week... when you have a backlog of mending and cooking, when you have hardly got time to stop to pee — and yet here I am, disregarding all, firmly convinced I will finish a reasonable letter to you in this next ½ hour while two children sleep and one is playing under the table!

*

I hope you received the plants and that they were healthy and lasting ones — hopefully one that flowers and one maidenhair fern, but they couldn't really promise anything. I can't remember what I wrote on the little white card so long ago, but I do remember that it was completely inadequate. That day in the florists shop was one of the times when the fact of your going hit me hard. I had to write something to you on a card as though you had gone — you hadn't yet gone, but I realized you would. And so I sat there, tears flowing, paralyzed, unable to write a word. The poor lady who was helping me was very patient — I remember I cried all the way home. Only later did I realize that the 24th was the day of the conjunction... (A mutual friend) said it was a day when the old "could come into relation with the new." That makes me especially glad about the flowers arriving on that day — surely it's not totally insignificant — it can't be just chance. "What wisdom works unknown to us behind our actions," etc. I do not doubt that our relationship is living and will continue to grow. — I pray that the plants did not arrive dead and diseased — especially after writing all this! And I do feel so close/connected to your new life and challenges and tasks — and will be with you as you build what you intend to build.

I know I will miss you and the day-to-day warmth of your friendship and support and the working together. But I know, too, that I can bear that. Amazing as it was to me at moments, I did not shatter into a million pieces — I continued to walk, talk, breathe, laugh even and do all the things I do. There were some moments when feeling the emptiness, I wondered where our relationship had gone — cut off, disappeared into a black hole of nothingness — totally gone. But then I knew that could not be and slowly already I feel it growing, stretching towards new ways and forms. So although I know there will be hundreds of moments when I'll expect you to be there, at least within reach of a telephone call, and you won't be, and it will be hard at those moments, I do know it's possible — and I do trust.

I wonder whether I'll ever get used to (your having moved away). It's obviously not only your destiny which has brought this pain into my life — and I cannot pretend it isn't pain. It belongs to our friendship and my life and destiny, too. That I know, and it isn't just meaningless... I realized in those days (before you left) how much I would miss (your husband) too — and how uncertain it made me feel that he would not be around. Seeing him, knowing him, I always felt I knew what my work was at a very deep level. Will I know it alone? Can I carry it alone? And that, I know, is blind and ridiculous, because there are many people here who carry the kind of work I do. And yet, I wail to the universe, why can't I work with you (both)? (My husband) was so good and strong in those days — like an angel...

Trying to find exactly where the pain was, I found it so many places, but I wondered whether there is not also a kind of etheric wound. All the memories and habits and patterns of our friendship and our working together. What do you think? Thinking about that, it then made sense why I have had a recurrent dream of your going — since you left. It's always complicated and fretful and not very satisfactory. — How could it be? — It's usually of you and (your husband) and the children packing or cleaning out your house or something. In my dream it's as though I keep trying to get it right, to see it clearly — to understand it — and stand it — and find a peace with it. But so far I can't get it to be very peaceful or clear or ordered. Strange, I hardly ever dreamt of you before, but now I have had many dreams.

*

I can remember beginning a letter to you some months ago, trying to do justice to this 33rd year — trying to explain how undermining it is to find one suddenly doubts oneself, sees all the inner shit that has somehow managed to stay submerged fairly comfortably since 18 or 20. And suddenly I remembered reading similar laments from you around the time you were 33 and I thought — it's probably all too familiar, and abandoned the letter. But herein certainly

hinges one of the chief difficulties in maintaining correspondence. Somehow, because it's impossible in a letter to
do justice to all the ins and outs of one's mental and emotional strugglings — and growth — one gets stuck on the
outward visible signs of life, and sometimes the inner struggle or growth can be mirrored there, but not always as that
kind of thing is often more mirrored in inactivity. On one
level, my life is always OK — but I can say that with full
knowledge that on another, I can be struggling and that it
is sheer hell. Also, because I know these things pass, I am
always reluctant to freeze them in time and send them off
to someone else who might have to wait three months to
hear how it all turned out and that is only if I remember to
include that detail.

Perhaps I should look at it this way — I am always
so glad to have <u>any</u> news of you — I mean I don't think it
would matter if you spent a letter describing your attitude
to the laundry — In fact, on that point, it would probably help; as (your husband — *who had recently visited them*)
described your laundrying as similar to mine — isn't it the
most odious of tasks? — that perhaps I should change my
expectations of what I want to write to you. And just fire off
the trivia and let you read between the lines.

✳

I've sent the kids upstairs for a half an hour, and already I
hear signs of the peace breaking... There is always so much I

want to share with you and so little time to write, and I can't help but feel constricted by the form of communication possible. The art of letter-writing?! Since having your telephone number, I have been continually tempted. I'm sure one day I'll give in. I miss you and feel rather hopeless about it all at times. Looking over my notes, driving, ironing, in the middle of talking to someone, playing with the kids in the evening — a thousand moments it sweeps over me — the loss, a kind of heaviness. As though it's settled in for good, found a vacancy and claimed it. It sounds terrible… and it is in a way. Why and what for?

✳

1982

I am cleaning my desk, and 're-read' a letter of yours from August '78. I really like such a thing! It's wonderful to have time to write friends. Reading again your letter, your 'style' is coming into my room, your way of life, your active attitude towards life.

It is strange to realize, by reading your letter, how much I have lived 'withdrawn' the last years. I almost had forgotten our exchange through letters. I was surprised to read that I had brought all kinds of thoughts to you, and that you became excited about them. I feel in this moment as awakening from a long sleep, did I write anything? Did

I say anything? It seems so very far away, so long, long ago!! Strange, really strange!

What have I done these last years? I have felt lonely, very lonely. I have felt 'misunderstood' these last years. I knew: I have some friends in England, they know what I mean... But here it has been strange. These years I have learned to be silent, to live withdrawn, to just keep quiet.

During this period, I have threatened people with my way of doing/ speaking/ living... It is really strange to experience that people don't like you, or don't receive or accept you the way you are. I have experienced that my attitude is felt by others as 'too much.' 'Too much' of what? I don't know exactly, but it will be in the realm of: too much directed, too much pronounced, too much open, too much conscious of everything, too much expecting from others the same attitude. I have felt forced to withdraw, to be silent, to not say what I feel or think, to just listen and to just keep superficial.

This has been painful and sad. What does it mean that people don't want what you bring with you?? I am trying to get an answer to the question — what has been the meaning of this period?

Now, looking back I really can feel the meaning. I have had to learn to take myself outwardly not too seriously. How can I say this clearly? I had to learn to become independent. If I feel — know — things are important, I have to care for them and just wait until they can become fruitful. This must be independent from people in my surroundings.

I have had to learn to accept people who live a totally different way, and not interfere in their way of life.

I have had to learn that I only have the responsibility for my <u>own</u> changes, my <u>own</u> realization of an ideal. Keep quiet!! Keep quiet, slowly, just do it myself! Not wanting from others that <u>they</u> change so I could change <u>with</u> them. Independence!!! Looking back, I can feel positive now, finally, on this period. It has been a hard and unpleasant teaching/lesson. But probably and hopefully I won't forget this lesson too soon.

✳

I loved your visit, every moment of it. I regretted nothing, except that you did have to go again, and that there were hundreds of things, trivial and grand, that there was no time to do or say or be. I wonder how it has been for you going back home? Have you found touching England again has made it easier to call Detroit home? harder? no difference? I've tried to see if there is a difference for me, and I did realize this time that your work is there, but I always could see that and I can still argue a good case why it could be here.

Although that Saturday morning dash to the airport was sad and hard, and we didn't get to finish our coffee, I was so glad to have taken you… and sitting there in that plastic restaurant at the end I felt such a good quality, a depth and a lightness, something not at all sad, and forever on into the future. Maybe I just felt I met our friendship, with a history, a past but moving with infinite possibilities into the future, enduring and growing.

*

I'm so glad your letter arrived today. I have been thinking about you so often since you left, but also have been in such a boring blah state that I have felt I can scarcely make a pen move, let alone find anything worthwhile to write. So reading your letter and being <u>so glad</u> to hear from you, I thought if you could overcome whatever it is — that strange listless, aimless yucky state that descends after a busy time and when there is no immediate pressure — so could I! I can't promise you an exciting, thought-provoking letter, but anyway a hello.

(12 pages later)

What I said in the beginning about struggling with letters and short visits doesn't sound very clear, and I'm not sure even how to write, express exactly the feelings I struggled with after you left. In a way, writing this letter now frees me again from a kind of frozen feeling, not towards you, but to start writing again. I guess to let a relationship live and grow through sometimes being together and mostly writing and always thinking and carrying the other requires flexibility, a willingness not to cling to any forms and trust in the reality of the connection. I realized when you left I had in some part of me forgotten you would, of course, go again. Then

I felt I had 'wasted' some time — yet there must be time to waste too! And then I wondered how to begin to write again... well I guess I'll learn... The real sorrow and loss I think will always be there yet it's so real I accept it completely, not with any downheartedness. And our friendship is such a joy and a gift for me. That's the other side, so I'm not really moaning.

*

I'll try to bring this long and rambling letter (**turned out to be 32 pages!**) to an end tonight so I can post it and so you'll know I am thinking of you and have not abandoned you — or vanished from the face of the earth. But the — one of the — horrid things about letters is that I have to fill it with me and can't know right now about you, how you are, what you are doing, thinking, feeling. Sitting here, curled up on the sofa writing away, I feel so close to you, but still I can't know what's happening in your life. I hope the sadness you were feeling is gone.

It pains me that I can't share everything with you, all my silly and profound thoughts. I hardly share them with anyone anymore, so I hardly know them. And, the other side of it is that I so miss the challenge and inspiration of your thoughts... I so wanted to talk with you for hours about the conference and all the ideas alive there. I burned and wept with them all, but I feel like all that remains is soggy ashes. Yuck. Still I feel I need to learn to keep things alive and let them grow and develop on my own. I feel too, more and more, this is a time for aloneness, inwardness, even loneliness — and silence?! — and withdrawal — in some ways — after so may years of rich exchange and friendship. I do know this time totally belongs to me — is part of my destiny. So when will I stop complaining?

＊

It is later — much. After your telephone call and your long letter. It seems like days that I've been trying to get back to writing, but there haven't been many free moments. How can I share with you all that happens, that I want to share, from the most trivial to the most profound. I suppose I must gradually learn discrimination — and learn that it can't be the same. But that's hard.

＊

I'm still dreaming a lot, and remembering them. (My husband) says because my moon node's coming up (**see note Chapter 4, page 179**). I dream a lot about people (at work) — and so much of you and (your husband). Tell him that whenever I meet him in my dreams I am <u>so glad</u> to see him — I always run up and embrace him. The warmth of feeling is the main impression and it lasts, lingers on into the day after I've woken up. But sometimes it's all so real that I just feel a kind of despair when I realize it's been a dream, and you are still far away.

What you wrote about tears and tear — as in wide open — and the etheric wound and boundary you felt, I found helpful. And I had just been reading your lecture notes on relationships about seeing and accepting the pain, without going down and under with it. And then your letter brings it in a different way, but the same, too. It's all true. Yet what do you do about a heavy heart? Where is the balance between recognizing it, and living through it, and not just covering it up and hiding it away, and getting on with what calls you forward, and being open to all that is around? If we are hurt, can we accept it and stay open instead of closing ourselves and hiding away so as not to be so vulnerable?

✳

Finally, here is the space I've been longing for, later than I expected. I feel completely limp in mind and body and hope I can rouse myself to share some of the last month or so with you. The trouble with my life these days is that when there is a moment, an hour, an evening when there is nothing 'to do,' I sit down and immediately fall asleep. I literally fell asleep at supper last night before a staff meeting, I think because finally, after a month and a half, the pressure was off for a moment! (The children) kindly let me stagger to the sofa and sleep for an hour while they cleaned up the kitchen!

✳

I have around me wonderful friends and colleagues, but our friendship and working together was different. Sometimes I can hardly bear life without our sharing. But I always knew it was a blessing so I haven't been completely shocked by the struggle without it. And, truly, in many ways I don't feel without. You — and (your husband and the children) too — are so much a part of my life, my days. Distance makes no difference to that. That is just the reality.

Why do I have these intense, forever relationships so far away? My life is so much richer through my friends — and I know that they too grow with my love — but why now long distance? Will it always be so — with only occasional hurried letters — and cards to remember a birthday! And still I feel so lucky to know this caring. Is it independence I must work on — standing alone, thinking alone, becoming creative alone. So hard for me — even as I know it never is really alone for all that I am and can be/do has been built by these others.

※

1983 – 1987

I feel sad that I've left you for so long without a response to your last letter, without news and support. I hope and trust that you know that I don't stop thinking about you when not writing, but I know <u>all</u> the support and talk can't be invisible. So, all of this is to say I think your idea about finding a weekly rhythm of writing letters is good, and I think we should try it, even if it has taken me one month just to say so. I also think we should just decide to do it and keep going as best we can even if we fail — not just give up the first time one or both of us fall short. I'll try to write on Tuesdays and post by Thursday.

I hope this doesn't become one more unfulfilled promise to myself, but since it's also to you, maybe I'll keep it. Do you still want to try? I like the possibility of not having to pick up everything — just taking one or two things and developing them and knowing that the next week there will be a chance to continue the conversation. Though I'm sure I'll try my best to fit in all the levels I can each week.

Could we learn to carry on with a theme, an idea, develop it, inspire each other through letters? Your letters often inspire me, but then I don't respond and the moment, the possibility is gone, or hard to recover. I also get inspired while writing to you, but often there is so much to say I find it hard to push through and really carry it further. We both are terrible at really describing the work we have been doing, the questions we meet, etc. because there is always <u>so much</u> to fill in. But with Spring in the air all things seem possible so let's try.

*

When I picture you in the evening, as I did last night, I often meet — and try to support and strengthen — your vulnerability and openness that goes with all your strength and capacity to give so much to others. I love both sides, but know the one is often not very visible to people, so I hope you are finding enough protection and that you aren't too lonely.

It was wonderful, having finally carved out the space for this letter, to receive your letter this morning. Thanks. But I don't know between what two non-existent minutes you wrote it. It exhausts me just to read what you have been busy with, so I do wonder how you are. I know from many conversations now that I am not the only one who had become ill from sheer exhaustion. So please be careful. Will next term be easier? or just as full? Can you cut out anything? And <u>go</u> to parties at <u>other</u> people's houses?!

I'll write you more thoughts as soon as I have a few thoughts.

(My husband) thinks that whatever is going on (a lingering illness) it is related to my missing you. He said it may be delayed grief. Well, I'm sure it's not that — because my grief certainly was not delayed or repressed. But it may be related to full speed in a lot of work that we shared — and do still share — but without the refreshing stimulating supporting exchange and interchange. Something (a mutual friend) said seems connected — "You should do some new work and research and find a friend to share it with." Well this lack of someone to truly share all the various levels may be related to my exhaustion. But so — I have to go on. How can we finally understand the meaning of this separation? I feel so selfish even asking, because for me there are many fewer dimensions to this than for you. Yet still it seems to spread out, influencing so much, and I want to understand. Please don't take this on as though, because, you left, I'm ill. It's not like that — you know that don't you?

(continuing letter, two days later)

What I've said in this letter, and what I said on the phone about maybe a connection between your move and this illness — do you understand there is no blame? How can I express it? I've never felt other than that separation was 'my destiny,' and I have been able to totally acknowledge it, almost love it, at that level while at the same time suffer it, wish it away, long for it to be otherwise, and mostly try to understand it and live with it.

✳

I cannot bear another month to begin, and I still have not written to you. I don't think I have ever been so totally absorbed by the physical side of life. I struggle for five minutes of reflection only to find myself falling asleep. And yet it must be done, and letter writing is a good place for it. I am sorry to have got into such a bad state of mind, so that I cannot even write the letters I want to write, let alone those which must be done.

✳

I must stop, or I'll fall asleep. This is, of course, nothing like what I intended to write, but I'll mail it, because it's something.

✳

And thank you for your strengthening thoughts. I truly feel your care and support. I know it and trust it and it helps me to bear this strange time.

✳

I hope you have a wonderful Christmas together... that you have peace and rest and recovery from such a busy term. And (your husband) too. I don't know if I'll ever get better at writing, but I do think of you all so much — of who you are who I love, of your work and aims, which I also love. I know the Life Center still struggles, yet I do not doubt it is what is truly needed there and so many places today — centers of life and nourishment and hope for people. So I pray that 1984 will bring new possibilities....

*

I find it sad, too, that I haven't been able to sit down with you at all this year. It's amazing that it's already over a year since you were here. It's gone so fast, and yet so much has happened — it feels like many years. I feel, as you expressed so well in your letter, that I continue to miss you, your friendship and colleagueship that extends to all levels, and that I can trust, yet I also accept the loss. It is a loss, and nothing changes that, and I do believe I am still struggling with it. And that's important, too. It's not a meaningless sadness or loss — I guess it's necessary, but I can't help myself hoping that when I've worked through my side, and you've learned and done whatever you have to learn and do, you'll come back!... But you know I also wish you and (your husband) to find what you truly want and need to do there or anywhere.

*

Your wonderful, long letter was waiting for me when I came back from holiday on Saturday. I wish I could do the same for you. I intended to write you from Cornwall — as well as to read several novels and several lectures, write many other letters, etc... Just as you describe, my not writing increases the intensity with which I think of you, dream of you, long to share more and more with you — until I cannot bear the gap any longer.

＊

I think in my life I have tried to work with the acceptance of separation and death, but sometimes I don't think I have come very far, and in the face of it I find it hard not to be sad or fearful. (A friend's) illness is a real challenge for me in this respect — really on so many different levels. I have had days where I am continually overcome by weeping and days of great confidence and hope. Also days of anxiety and worry. But he himself, even in this illness, continues to be a tremendous teacher. His spirit is so amazing, so full of joy and confidence, so lacking in doubt or self-pity or self-ishness of any kind. So strong and trusting in the spiritual world. So courageous.

＊

Maybe if I begin this <u>before</u> I get your long letter, you'll get a letter from me! Once I get yours, I will be overwhelmed with so many things I want to say to you, that it's impossible for me to quieten myself enough to sit down and write… and so I won't… and then life at 100 mph intervenes and months pass and my sense of frustration increases… I'm sure you know all of this pretty well!

You know you wouldn't believe this… For the last hour (my toddler) has been playing quietly by himself. I've prepared supper, and have these few minutes to sit down and write. So, what happens? I look up, and there is the boy, in the middle of the kitchen bench, onto which he has climbed with the aid of two chairs, about to electrocute himself with the kettle. That was at the end of the word 'letter,' in the 2nd line. I put him down, threatened him with worse than electrocution if he did it again — see *Lifeways* for creative discipline! — and sat down to write some more. Next time I looked up, he had the window cleaner — laundry door left open again! — and was spraying (his older sister's) legs as she sat reading. I removed the window cleaner, shut the laundry door, pacified (his sister), threatened (him) AGAIN, and sat down to write. Next time I looked up that little turd had the sugar bowl. By then I was up to 'well' and wondering whether I should just give up. I decided I'd press on, so I told him in no uncertain terms that I meant to write and that he would sit and PLAY. And he is, quite contentedly now.

(And then after two more sentences the letter ends for a few days!)

※

I resolved to write to you when we got to the beach. I forgot, of course, what it does to my increasingly still body of bones to crouch over a writing pad in the sand, or outside the tent. We still haven't run to such luxuries as camping chairs, or tables. Economic sanctions and some sort of last ditch non-consumerism, no longer arrogant but slightly frantic — the "who needs all of that clutter," which I suspect is our way of maintaining a sort of footloose and fancy freeness, or illusion of same — in the face of ever mounting evidence to the contrary with our houseful, family-full, job-full lives. I also forgot — of course I have denied that the place where my pathological sanguinity is most clearly manifest is in my perpetual, <u>stupid</u> optimism — how difficult it is to collect oneself amid the expanse of sea and sky, the offshore shrieks of bathers, the inshore demands of sand castle builders, the smell of chips and a very, very dead lungfish that contrives to be upwind of us, wherever we sit. Still, it's nice here.

Now we've talked — and way too long for your phone bill, but of course never too long from all other points of view. But I have in the end a real sorrow that I don't manage to 'talk' to you regularly through letters. We always have had plans of how to keep in touch about our work — shared work in so many areas — and our lives, but I never manage it. And then a gap grows — not in essence, in my heart and thoughts, but actually practically. There are so many things that I want to share and work through with you that just build up and are tucked away forever. Is it unrealistic to want to continue to work and share together? Am I holding on to a false dream — or if not, <u>how</u> to do it? I feel pretty depressed by my own inability to do what I want.

I have had an active ache since your birthday that it passed without even a letter, or a card, to tell you how much I was/am thinking of you. It was one of those times — I'm sure you know them all too well, my friend, that by waiting to find the 'right' thing to send, you find nothing at all, but because you're sure to find it tomorrow, and then it will only be a little bit too late, you don't write to say it will be late. And tomorrow and tomorrow and tomorrow and then it's a week, a fortnight — a month. And the ache grows, and the consternation at what you've inadvertently — ? — done, grows, and the distress that you're still as disorganized as you've always been... or more so, grows... And in amongst all this you have eight fundraisers; a friend who has a baby and gets the worst post-natal depression you've ever seen; a friend who becomes pregnant, who is single, 33 — of course — and doesn't want the child/can't see any way to keep the child/yet agonizes over abortion and the spiritual/karmic implications;... and a house to clean and a family to be there for; and a job to do, and four new people arriving at (work — a center for people with disabilities) to be embraced and encountered and introduced. Throw in an open day, a fete, another fete for the Waldorf School, and the acceleration of end of the year — three separate plays to rehearse — and a few unrelated emotional stresses and you have the beginnings of a context in which to place the ache I originally referred to! It is ridiculous, isn't it? — I'm so guilt ridden that if there is a space, I'm afraid I'm lazy and fill it up! I'm afraid of my inner life? Or lack thereof? Or abundance thereof? And or all of that seems possible, and I'm sure there are others as well.

∗

I received your letter shortly after arriving in California after 13 years in England!...It was incredibly wonderful to receive your letter during my 'homecoming'. . . . I opened boxes of memories which had been stored before in San Francisco for such a long, long time. As you said in your letter — so much has happened! I found the letter in storage that I received from you right before I left for England in 1975 — when you were just starting with Ariadne, having... two children about the age mine are <u>now</u>! And now yours are in college — or almost....

EPILOGUE

Where Are We Now?

"These are such dear friends — so much a part of who I am — wonderful to feel that bond of love and real care and support between us. Life has moved on for all of us, yet what we shared together has given us such strengths — and I think we all feel we can touch back to our connections, whether we are near each other or not. I don't have the same ache of no longer being near — and yet I feel how they are who can still help me grow, help me face next steps — would keep me gently and lovingly to my real tasks. Can I let them do this even from afar — in my thoughts?"

The above quote is from my journal in the summer of 1986, after a visit with several of the letter writers in this book. It was written about the small group of women with whom I met regularly for seven years when I lived in England, and whenever possible since then. But, in truth, those words can be said about all the friends whose letters are included here.

My writer friends did not all know each other, although each of them knew at least one other besides me, and many knew several others very well. As stated earlier, counting me, there are words from twenty-one women in this book. I am in regular contact with most of these friends. Despite the marvels of modern technology, I have not been able to reconnect with two. Sadly, two others are no longer alive. We came originally from seven different countries, and are now spread through four of those plus two others, and right across the whole of the United States.

Most of us are now in our seventies, with a few who have already entered their eighties and one still in her late sixties. When we were writing these letters, we were young, educated, and optimistic about our futures. In 21st century terminology, we were privileged, not necessarily financially, but because we felt we had choices in our lives. Nevertheless, before the time of these letters, different ones of us had already experienced many of the difficulties that women world-wide, and of course many men as well, have long endured: economic hardship, parental alcoholism, single parents, gender restrictions on education, domestic abuse, divorce, sexual assault, prejudice, and the list could go on. In our relationships, we looked for and tried to encourage the best and the possible in each other.

We believed that times were changing and that we could follow our dreams. And we knew what we were receiving from our friendships.

In the decades since the letters were written, as would be the case with any grouping of twenty-one older women, we have experienced great joys and great sorrows. In some of our families there have been life-altering illnesses or traumatic accidents. There have been wrenching losses and remarkable recoveries. When I think about us as a 'whole,' I see that in our very individual ways, we have collectively met a broad range of life's offerings — gifts, challenge, success, hardship, disappointment, support, betrayal, delight, tragedy, fulfillment...Through our long lives, we have persevered and endured, learning all along about courage and resilience, trying ever and again to know ourselves more deeply and to be of service to our families, friends, communities and the broader world.

Four of my friends were not yet married when we began writing. Over the years there were eight divorces, but also there have been fifteen long marriages — some as a second one, including seven where a fiftieth anniversary has already been celebrated, or will be soon. Those of us who have been married for decades know the grace, the heartaches, the gifts, and the work of commitment. Those who have remained single have pursued lives of inspiring independence and adventure. I imagine that amongst us all, we have met, suffered, and tried to step beyond most of the challenges that relationships can bring.

Some of the letters show us experiencing the threshold of birth and growing with our young children. Those children are now mostly middle-aged — many considerably older than we were when we wrote our letters. These children stretched our hearts, challenged us at times to the very core of our being, and continue to inspire us in myriad ways. Many have become parents themselves and have blessed several of us with beloved grandchildren. A few of us are even great-grand-mothers. Yet even with this renewal of generations, our lives are now closer to the threshold of death than to birth. Some partners have died, some siblings, even an adult child, and a grandchild, and all of us can imagine the partings that lie ahead. The realities of aging are a factor of our daily lives.

Most of the writers have been on a long search to understand human life and development, both in our earthly existence and as part of a broader spiritual reality. Through the years, many deepened their commitment to inner work, often — but not only — on a foundation of ideas and practices from Rudolf Steiner. In several cases our work in the world grew out of our spiritual searching and our inner striving, for example as teachers, adult edu-cators, counselors or art therapists. Most of us are retired now, but we continue with part-time or volunteer work in our communities, as well as activism in a variety of social justice arenas. We have served on innumerable committees and boards over the years, and this goes on. Most are still active with artistic disciplines, such as drawing, painting, handwork, and writing. We are a collection of fairly serious women, although in different small groupings we still giggle with all the abandon of earlier days! All of us have continued to be interested in pursuing ideals that move our hearts, and we have tried in many different ways to serve a healthier, kinder and more peaceful world.

Generalizations about this collection of women can only give a fairly shallow picture. I am so grateful to Noela Maletz for suggesting that I ask my friends to write a brief life update. When I contacted the group, I received some immediate replies begging for a bit of extra time because one was going salmon fishing in Alaska, another was off to Italy, another to Greece, and still another to France. One was just leaving to meet with aboriginal women about questions of land use and spirituality. And several were busy with visits to grandchildren or memorials for parents or old friends — a picture of our activity now at both ends of life. Eventually I received letters from fifteen friends and was able to piece together something for two more. Some tell of times before we met or speak to the importance of our letters; all touch the years since our time of writing. The life-rich individualities of my friends radiate across the pages. I am very happy to be able to let my friends now speak in their own voices, finally with their names attached.

I am sharing these letter updates from my friends in roughly the order in which we came to know each other over the years. But I am breaking that pattern right at the start, by placing words from **Noela Maletz** first, since the idea for this sharing was hers.

You have called this book, *I Give You My Word*, and it's true, I did, we all did. But you kept the words, and because you did, you are returning to each of us those long ago past selves that we barely remember, but which we recognize with fondness and a smile, or sometimes a wince. Each of us gave you ourselves in words, and with love and trust that you would see us.

I wrote out loud on paper in order to see myself, my children, my partner, my life. And to share it with you. Through the lens of you, I wrote to discover the meaning and purpose that I longed to feel beneath the ordinariness of the ordinariness. When I sat down to knit together all the disparate bits that made the whole garment of that day, month or week, I became the creator, but only because you were there, the co-creator of that moment by your receiving of it. Sometimes I needed to write, to relieve the unbearable pressure of noticing everything. It was always therapeutic. The satisfaction of encapsulation, the joy of exchange, the challenge of forming a thought on paper when half brain dead... The distillation of days, the long view of what could be — all of this would have passed, unseen and unwritten had there not been a reader, a beloved presence on the other side of the world or the continent, to whom I wrote. Thank you.

Beyond this diarizing, this noting, this sharing, why did we do it? Why were those threads of connection so important? I began putting myself on paper early: pen pals were fashionable and encouraged and in the apostrophe to the world that Australia felt like in the 50's and 60's, it was a way of reaching out to the world beyond this island, and calling it in. My first real pen pal was a Girl Guide in New Zealand and I still remember her address, to this day, and the joy of receiving her simple letters and the ordeal of thinking of something to say beyond "I did this, and then we did that." So I began early, and had had a fair bit of practice by the time it came to leaving England in 1975 with a baby in Christa's carry cot, a husband and the hope of Bio-Dynamics in the Southern Hemisphere.

Australia was a long way from Forest Row. When I wrote to you, I wrote to all of us who had shared in Ariadne, who had wondered together about the meaning of everything, and who somehow, I knew dimly, were doing their own version of finding their ways in the world with children, marriages, jobs and destiny. I knew you would get it. I knew you would reply, with questions, thoughts and challenges of your own. We were alive to our worlds through each other. Thank you.

And now, I am seventy, and you are even older, which even if I had had time or inclination, I could not have imagined when I was 30. But here we are, still writing, still talking, threading our thoughts and endeavours on strings that stretch between us. You have often said to me, sort of laughing, "how come everyone I know has become a counsellor?" Great question!!! I wish I could begin to answer it. But what I do know, is that I cannot think of anything in my life at this age, that could be more enlivening, more enriching, more sobering. I love my work. I love the people whose stories I share. I love the windows into lives and the wisdom they hold open. I love the sense that they, too, give me their words, their lives, their selves, with the same trust with which I gave mine to you, and you to me. We are each, in our own ways, following the trail guide of mystics, holding onto the threads of biography. We were wise to invoke Ariadne.

With love and gratitude, Nx

∗

Noela mentions pen pals in her childhood, and so I make space here for my older sister who was such a central part of my life since childhood. I also want to remember a childhood friend with whom I wrote early letters and who became like another sister in my family. Sadly, they have both died, but their words are in this book, and their presence in my heart continues.

When my sister, **Linda Norris**, was first diagnosed with cancer in her late fifties, it was a hard blow. Even though we lived several hours away from each other, we decided to begin a daily writing practice. Each evening one of us would call the other, and we would agree on some word that had appeared in our day — *opening, love, laundry, doorknob, balance, comfort, honesty, button*…. The words we chose could be grand or simple, but we would hang up and each write for up to ten minutes. Then we would reconnect and read what we had written. Between us, we would have really entered the chosen word. The writing was spontaneous but also a kind of meditation — we often ended up going places we could never have imagined. We shared this writing practice for a whole year, almost every day. It was healing, enriching, and profoundly important to each of us, and to our relationship.

Linda died in 2007, so I could not ask her to write something about herself. And yet, I wanted her voice to be part of this epilogue. One day I had the idea to look back at our writings and see if we had perhaps written about *words*. We didn't use computers for this — all the writing was by hand. Linda's pieces were not very organized, she left several half-used notebooks and many scraps of loose paper, some with grocery lists on the other side, all stuffed into a worn cloth bag from the Museum of Fine Arts in Boston that she gave me soon before she died. As I began rummaging through the bag looking for what she might have written about *words*, my hand pulled out a small yellow pad that was on the bottom of the bag under everything else. The first few pages had some lists, times of doctors' appointments, a notation about shitake tea, and then blank pages. I thought, "I could actually throw this away," but for some reason I kept leafing through the pages. Linda must have been guiding me for after several blank pages, I came upon the following letter, written in pencil, in what looked like one hurried inspiration without editing. Linda actually lived for several years after writing this and later wrote other farewell pieces closer to the time of her death, but I am sure I never saw this one before. It had been waiting since 2001, to now be part of this book. There was no greeting, but I imagine it was addressed to her world, and in particular to the people in her town.

I always hoped when I made it to the obituary column, it would say Linda Norris, 83 — but it looks like it's going to say Linda Norris, 59. **(She actually lived to be almost 65.)**

I have ovarian cancer that has spread. Yes, it is most unpleasant. But my most recent year and a half has been a huge gift. I changed my ping-pong ball way of eating to a healing macrobiotic diet. I lost 70 pounds by giving up meat, dairy, oil, sugar. I learned so much and felt so good — lots of energy. Took care of granddaughters — went international folk dancing on Tuesdays. At one point I started tap lessons. And of course, I shopped — and here I would like to offer great thanks to so many in town who became my extended 'family.' even though they didn't know it. **(She then names thirty-five different shops and restaurants!)** How many wonderful people there are in our town. If I was sad or mad or lonely, they would put positive energy into my day, and I would simply feel better.

Besides people and food I've loved crafts, candlelight, flowers, and animals — such dear friends — and music.

Recently I've been working on developing an

alternative healing center for Great Barrington — to be called, The NOAH Center, standing for New Opportunities of Alternative Healing. It's been so exciting to plan it — with of course lots of help and ideas from friends. I wish it could still happen. **(It did.)** There is so much work to be done on this front.

I want to thank you all for these past 20 years of you allowing me to develop to myself here — supporting me — helping me learn. So thank you, thank you. And my husband Bob — God — he is such a fine man. Please help him.

Be well, eat well, breathe well — sing — do nice things and feel good.   Love, Linda

*

Linda had a phrase she often used, a combination of words that she somehow made sound like one long word: "the-dead-and-the-angels." She lived with a certainty that those who have died and also the angelic world are somehow always around us, available to us if we are open to the working of spirit, and not too distracted by self-preoccupation or sensory bombardment, or bound by the materialism of our present age. Finding her letter as I did felt like a true confirmation of her belief in the help of the ever-present dead-and-the-angels. I could almost hear her gently laughing at my amazement.

I had another 'sister,' **Tessa Chao**, whose words are also included in this book and who sadly also died of cancer in 2014. Tessa and I met in seventh grade, when we both lived in Santiago, Chile. Her father was with the Taiwanese Embassy. My father was in the Antarctic, and my mother had decided that since he would be gone for so long, she, Linda and I should have the adventure of a year in South America. Although I lived in Chile for only that one year, Tessa and I stayed in touch through letters. Then a few years later her father was transferred to Saudi Arabia and she was to be sent to boarding school in London. I asked my parents if she could come live with us instead, and they agreed. She became a much-loved member of our family. After high school and college, she went on to complete a PhD and then worked as a research biochemist.

Two days after I found the letter from Linda, I had a phone call with Tessa's husband who recently moved out of the house he and Tessa had lived in for many years. With a chuckle he said that in the sorting and packing he had found a gift for me from Tessa, all wrapped for Christmas. There were no other wrapped presents with it. I could only think that like Linda's letter, this might hold some special greeting, a final updating word from Tessa, coming now almost five years after her death. When I received the present (a very nice paring knife) a few days later, I smiled in wonder to read on the card in Tessa's characteristically neat handwriting, *"Just what you need (like a hole in the head), Love, Tes."*

The-dead-and-the-angels indeed — words that I needed from my sisters, coming right through that invisible hole in the top my head!

*

My box of letters also included words from two college friends with whom I have been lucky enough to stay in contact since the fall of 1963 when we met as freshmen at Tufts University.

Marcia Putnam was my college roommate for four years, and we have been writing to each other — sporadically — for over fifty years. In fact, I can remember the first letter she wrote me in the summer of 1963, to introduce herself once we had heard we would be roommates but before we met. As the pages of funny stories and deep, complex questions tumbled out of the overstuffed envelope, I knew immediately this was someone I would love. Through changing careers, growing families, continental and international moves — including some overlapping time in England — and huge, challenging life events, we have never lost contact. Marcia is now engaged with her family in recording their own intense life story, and so instead of writing a brief update, she sent me a few of her favorite quotes that speak to how she thinks and who she is now.

First are the ending lines of T.S. Eliot's "Little Gidding," from *Four Quartets*, which I remember Marcia

loving when we were still in college, but which of course
have layers more meaning now that we are older:

With the drawing of this Love and the voice of this Calling

We shall not cease from exploration
And the end of all our exploring
Will be to arrive where we started
And know the place for the first time.
Through the unknown, unremembered gate
When the last of earth left to discover
Is that which was the beginning;
At the source of the longest river
The voice of the hidden waterfall
And the children in the apple-tree
Not known, because not looked for
But heard, half-heard, in the stillness
Between two waves of the sea.

Quick now, here, now, always--
A condition of complete simplicity
(Costing not less than everything)
And all shall be well and
All manner of thing shall be well
When the tongues of flames are in-folded
Into the crowned knot of fire
And the fire and the rose are one.

Marcia wrote to me of the "many poems I love… all my life. I have kept them by my side as sustenance throughout my life from a young age." **And then she quoted words from William Faulkner which almost sound like a life motto, one that definitely needs to be sounded today, for all of us:**

So, never be afraid. Never be afraid to raise your voice for honesty and truth and compassion, against injustice and lying and greed. If you, not just you in this room tonight, but in all the thousands of other rooms like this one about the world today and tomorrow and next week, will do this, not as a class or classes, but as individuals, men and women, you will change the earth.

And finally a quote she sent from George Bernard Shaw:

Life is no brief candle to me. It is a sort of splendid torch which I have got a hold of for the moment, and I want to make it burn as brightly as possible before handing it on to future generations.

Here are Marcia's own closing words about Shaw's statement: "I think this quote says it all for me — I have always felt this way. I just want to take hold of every bit of this life that I have — this splendid torch."

*

Although always staying in touch, Nancy Lippincott and I had not seen each other for decades until spring 2018, when she and her husband stopped by our home for a visit. As we launched into deep conversation, it felt like no time had passed at all. Nancy was the person who had the idea that my husband-to-be and I should meet, way back in 1966. During our recent visit, she described that idea coming to her as a kind of inspiration, something she just had to set in motion. Thank you Nancy for our long friendship and for that karmic spark!

Signe's invitation to write an up-dated bio-byte sounded a bit like an invitation to write an epilogue: after our child-rearing years passed, so also passed the conflicting tensions between family and community life. And we all live happily ever after.

In some ways, this is true. Our sons have grown, graduated, married, and found agreeable employment. They no longer live near us, so time together is always precious--and also dynamic and fun. They have been a source of strength for us, and we are grateful for it. On the flip side, although they are both stably employed now, they realize that the career-long employment known to their father and grandfathers has vanished from their world. They are expecting to adapt to the "gig" economy.

My husband and I cherish the "golden years" of retirement. Now well past the divide and conquer stage of child rearing, we choose to do most of our activities together. Our community activities fall into three areas: music, education, and political reform. Our personal activities include time with friends and family, traveling, attending concerts and plays, reading, enjoying nature, and organizing our photos into memory books and movies.

Yet there is a flip side here as well. We have also entered the more somber age where infirmities begin to creep up and friends begin to pass away. Fortunately, so far, we remain basically healthy and active, even as we mourn some friends who have left us too soon.

Most of all we enjoy the balance retirement allows.

We value both "going out" to travel, social events, community responsibilities and "coming in" to quiet times, reading, studying, devising personally important projects, and just plain sitting on our backyard deck watching fireflies blink to each other before we all settle down for the night.

*

My friendship with **Karen Gierlach** is approaching fifty years and has seen our families sharing houses in both the US and England, then years of living far apart but always re-connecting when we can, and regularly exchanging ideas about our evolving interests over the decades.

In the years since writing those letters to Signe, my life has been a mixture of ups and downs: satisfying, frustrating, joyful, challenging, exciting, and sometimes quite hard.

My first marriage dissolved after 13 years, at a time when my children were still in grade school. After my divorce was finalized, I moved away from the community which we'd become part of for 10 years. For the next seven years I was a single mother, without child support from my children's father. Luckily my children attended the school where I taught full-time, so logistics were doable. We survived those meagre years quite well, thanks to good friends and understanding colleagues, as well as two supportive sets of grandparents.

After a few short-term, dead-end relationships, I connected deeply and permanently with my now second husband. After seven more years of dating and living in separate houses we become confident and clear enough about daring to marry for a second time. Soon after our wedding we were called to another Waldorf community and spent 6 years working in a new school there together.

Because of chronic migraines and thanks to my ever-supportive husband, I eventually began to work part-time and thereafter only as a volunteer in organizations that interested me. First, I became trained as a hospice volunteer and visited the bedsides of many patients. I found this a most fulfilling occupation, particularly because my main role was to listen and provide whatever was needed in each situation. This was a complete reversal of the way I had been working for many years, always planning ahead, following an agenda or completing a to-do list. I also worked as a volunteer with refugees, with new immigrants, providing information in several languages to visitors in Yosemite National Park, and planting and protecting native plants.

Related to hospice work, two years ago I joined our local Threshold Choir. After singing in large choirs all my life, beginning in high school, I now sing in very small groups at the bedsides of terminally ill patients. Singing in an intimate setting became very personally meaningful for me when I sang at the bedside of my very old and dying father. Two years later, alas, I did that same for my younger sister during the last weeks of her life.

In my early forties, I attended a biography and social art workshop led by Signe and Chris and was quite intrigued by Rudolf Steiner's picture of human development in the adult years. Once I was no longer working full-time, I was encouraged by a friend to offer biography workshops myself. I began studying and ever more observing the lives of others as well as my own. Since then I have facilitated many workshops, also in other countries, and to an ever-wider audience. I once had the joy of leading a workshop attended by Arab and Israeli Waldorf parents and teachers in Israel. I hope to find more opportunities to bring together people from different faiths and political perspectives through the social art of interactive biography experiences. "An enemy is someone whose story you haven't heard" is one of my favorite quotes. I partly attribute this particular interest of mine to growing up bilingual in post-war Germany as a child of English parents. Fortunately for me, I was never made to feel that I was growing up among our former enemies and was too young, initially, to know what the war had been all about. Learning to hate another group of people is clearly something that has to be taught.

Today I am grateful that my children are living in places they enjoy and working at jobs of interest to them. I have not been blessed with grandchildren, but do like spending time here and there with the grandchildren of others. I continue to study Rudolf Steiner's works and try to apply what I learn in my daily life. This provides me with a perspective and trust in the spiritual forces that support us, when dealing with both the global political challenges and in daily life.

I like being of support to others needing help. The others might be older or less mobile than me, or at times much younger and dealing with life issues that I recognize as similar to my own from years past. I try to understand rather than too quickly judge the younger generations and the rapidly changing world in which we live now. I am grateful that I had parents and Waldorf teachers who took an interest in me and thereby nurtured my interests in what was happening around me in the world.

All in all, life is calmer and easier now and I have grown a little wiser through the many mistakes I have made. I have also become ever more grateful for all the support and the lessons I have received from others throughout my life. That said, there is plenty more to learn and develop. And so, the journey continues....

*

Very soon after arriving in England in 1973, I met **Christa Kaufmann** through our little boys in nursery school. Soon we were having passionate conversations about life as women in the beginning days of the women's movement. We felt the importance of what was stirring, and we wanted to connect this with our interest in spiritual questions. A year later we launched a women's group together. A few months after the start of that first group, Christa returned to the US with her family. Since then we see each other when we can, which is not often, but the heart-bond between us endures.

"Where there is a lot of pain, good things can grow." This is a quote by Alan Watts, a well-known Zen philosopher, who witnessed my marriage struggles in the early 70's while living in Santa Barbara. I will say that he was not only right, but it was as though he foresaw elements of my marriage, and my growth into my future.

What was to come, I could not have imagined. My naive, innocent perspective of wife-hood had been tested over and over again. I was deeply committed to a spiritual life practice, to the extent that I understood what that meant. However, after a series of self-help therapies, support groups, uncertainty, illusions, and misadventures to create and live within a true, healthy relationship, I felt that I had failed, and ended my marriage of 20 years.

So, out of necessity, I reached into a pool of self-reliance, courage, love for adventure, and perhaps an illusionary sense of self-confidence. This opened the gates to a fascinating, and rewarding chapter of life. I had learned a new professional skill, which I entered into with enthusiasm and success. From my kitchen, as wife, and mother, always dedicated to serve my family, I found myself in a totally different world, directing national and international campaigns that would raise millions of dollars for worthy causes. I sometimes wondered why, and how it was, that I suddenly met with world leaders, and celebrities I had only heard about, read about, and who were now in my life, all be it, in a temporary, but significant way.

While involved in this remarkable, and different life phase, I acknowledged wholeheartedly, that I felt blessed, privileged, and interested in my own biography. I had cheated death four times by the time I had reached the age of four while living in Germany during World War II, had lived in exotic places in the world after leaving my home country, and felt interested and enthusiastic about every aspect of life that I encountered along the way.

Much later, after my retirement, I felt more than blessed to have three of my five children, with six of my 12 grandchildren, living within a short distance from where I had settled in the San Francisco area. I thought often, how very lucky we all were to have each other.

Then it happened. The nightmare of nightmares crashed its way into my life, and into the life of our family. A call from my oldest daughter. "Mom, are you alone? Sit down, I have some terrible news"... my heart froze. "We have lost two members of our family." Afraid to tell me who it was, and only after my terrified, yet strangely calm, insistence, she told me that my eldest son and his daughter had drowned in Hawaii, as I was innocently going about my day, 2,719 miles to the East. Five months later, my children's father also died.

Now life has become a new experience. Each moment is now strangely richer, more meaningful, more demanding of truth and appreciation. There is no more need to color unpleasant realities with politically correct attitudes, words or deeds. Only a true expression, and profound experience of life, and of living it.

*

Ellen Robin was a young student at Emerson College who saw the notice announcing the first women's group and participated in that year of exploring together the many questions we all shared. After a couple of years in England, when she would often drop by our house bringing good cheer and maybe a delicious, newly-invented dessert, she returned to the States and eventually settled in California.

When Signe asked me to write a few paragraphs about myself for the epilogue of this book, I found myself wondering what I was actually like in my twenties, during the years I was involved in our women's group and when I wrote the letters she has excerpted. I know that despite my self-doubt and overall naiveté, I was energetic, curious, adventurous, and idealistic. I showed up in Signe's life in England with a college education and certification to teach elementary school kids and more specifically, hospitalized children and kids with physical disabilities. Aside from the training for my chosen profession, I was turned on in 1969 by only one class in my liberal arts education: Women in American Society, taught by the brilliant feminist lawyer and later Episcopal priest Pauli Murray, and one of the first classes in Women's Studies anywhere. But at 23, I felt utterly unprepared for what I considered the foundation of my future work: some understanding of what it means to be or to have a disabled or very ill child. Therefore, I refused to apply for teaching jobs and instead, made my living for a short time catering beautiful desserts to restaurants around Harvard Square in Cambridge.

When I got to England, at the urging of my childhood friend Lisa who is another letter-writer in this group, I discovered, as she had predicted, schools with a completely different approach to what "handicapped" or "special needs," never mind childhood means. Imagine! — in teaching a child, the concepts of love, soul, incarnation, remedy could be just as critical as assessment, evaluation, defect, medication. Over my short time in England, with the support of other women trying to figure out how to live and work, be mothers and lovers, I can see that I gained the confidence to live my life and do my work as a teacher, cook, and administrator my own way — with my own eclectic values, passionately, and certainly on fire. My world had opened up.

From there, I was ready to say yes to many opportunities that have punctuated my life. In England, I took on a huge cooking/catering job running the kitchens at a Waldorf school which fed 140 students and teachers every day. Later, I was asked to create and direct other new programs that I felt passionate about for children and families — for example, an elementary school for pediatric patients in Rhode Island Hospital and a supplementary religious school at my synagogue in northern California, my home for the past 38 years. And for up to 65 Jewish women, I am a coordinator for an annual, unique rustic retreat held in Mendocino County.

My husband Michael and I and our family have lived for 25 years on five acres with scores of fruit trees, olives for oil, and redwood and oak stands full of wildlife and firewood — and we have three sons. Raising three boys now dubbed Millennials and often feeling like an alien in my own house was probably my biggest challenge during those years when the emphasis was on girls'/women's empowerment. One of my kids astutely asked me in third grade: how come people think just because I'm a boy I'm going to grow up to be a jerk? What a good question to shock me into active focus on the need for well-rounded young men in our society!

Looking back now, I realize that while I did not follow one career path that I could graph as a slanted straight line, what I called the various splashes I've made could be better re-named seeds. Honestly, I like that term better; it's got less ego and implies a more promising future. Today is Election Day in the US, and I am holding my first grandchild Zadie Elaine. I will always hope that I've done enough.

Stephanie Cooper was also a participant in that first women's gathering that Christa and I called together, and she then continued as a member of the ongoing group, even after she moved to another part of England some years later. Several of us still come together when we can. I feel so grateful that when I manage to return to England, Stephanie and the others make space in their lives for our special days of meeting.

The other night at a supper party, I found myself sitting next to a young woman, well youngish, a similar age to my youngest daughter, Lissie. We asked each other the usual questions about work, family and how we came to be there. As we talked, I became very aware that all the issues and questions she was struggling with, were the same as mine in the 70s and 80s. Perhaps the only difference in this next generation is that they are older, having children later. Although she and her husband are accountants, she has given up that profession to write her first novel. So she balances that with

3 young children, and her husband working full time as the breadwinner.

I told her about *I Give You My Word*. She was very interested to hear about it and looks forward to reading it.

This encounter, after having read most of the content of the chapters in *I Give You My Word*, brought back to me quite powerfully, those struggles with relationship questions, bringing up children, the pressures of expectation in how you should meet challenges, questions of identity — who am I, where am I in the spectrum of masculine / feminine? What does that mean?

Coming together in our women's group in the 70s seemed the most exciting step to take, and our time together was the highlight of the week! As this work developed, some of us became more active in spreading the fruits of our intense time together.

I always felt more reticent about doing this and let my friends find their voice and 'go public.'

Eventually I gained the courage and confidence to find my way. After some diversions, I trained as an art therapist, and this was for me the most fulfilling of times, and continues to give me great satisfaction.

Who am I now? In many ways I feel secure, accepting that this is how life is, I cannot change the world, only the small things around me. But then I can slip into old patterns of taking on too many things in a sanguine way out of enthusiasm or wanting to help. I think I am still 40, but oh, the frustration of recognizing my limitations. That is a big learning curve, which has been speeded up recently by having an accident.

But what comes as I get older is a tremendous feeling of love and gratitude for all those who have helped me through the difficult times of my life. In particular, it has come from my sisterhood over decades of listening, sharing and supporting. Thank you!

*

Another member of the women's group that has met for so long is Dede Bark. In her words now she speaks about her second marriage and the home she and her husband created for an extended family of lively children. She also addresses the painful loss of her husband.

Reading the extracts from letters that Signe's many friends had written to her over the years takes me back to 1975 when I joined a Women's Group in Forest Row. At the time my husband and I were living there with our five children. For both of us it was our second marriage — to which we each had brought two children. A baby girl was soon born to us, thus completing our 'blended' family' and leading me to step down from my work at the Waldorf School where Peter and I had both been teaching.

Living close to the school, our home had always been a place for children to gather and it was not long before bedrooms had to be extended to enable two young boys to come to join us as boarding students. It was indeed a lively home, and when my husband returned at the end of the day, I greeted him over what always appeared to be a sea of children's heads. We felt really blessed that the children all got on so well together, but gradually I became aware that it was the back of Peter's head that I was becoming so familiar with as he later sat diligently working at his desk. The rare evenings when we were able to get away together were precious to us both and lead me to realize just how much I was missing the chance of having uninterrupted adult conversation with him!

Then came the invitation to join the Women's Group! Although I knew a few of the women who came together that first evening, there were others I had not met before. Once the meeting got under way, I caught a whisper of what was opening up for me and knew I had found something that I had been longing for. The diversity of backgrounds of those who had gathered together brought a richness to the themes that we explored, allowing an atmosphere of warmth and trust to develop — nurturing a space for feelings of empathy to grow.

We were caught up in our own journey towards consciousness-raising, and over the years many groups working from the same impulse, which we gave the name Ariadne, were formed throughout the world. It was an exciting time. Though many of our original group moved on, some of us, now in our seventies, have continued to meet when we can, offering support and loving care for each other through many phases of our lives.

From the start, I recognised how important becoming part of the Women's Group was in my life. I became involved with others in offering workshops on themes connected to our Ariadne work, as well as assisting in Biographical Workshops. This was all work that I loved so much and that later led me train as a Counsellor. In the meantime I returned to work alongside my husband at the Waldorf School. Our extended family continued to grow — finally leading us to move to a larger house. In many ways this was hard work, but everyone happily pulled together and when our youngest daughter started school she told her teacher that she had eight brothers!

Finally, as our older children — together with those who had now become so much a part of our family — set out on their own adventures, we moved once more to a smaller house. At first our home seemed strangely quiet, but we soon settled in with a sense of freedom and recognition that we were now able to follow up interests that had long been put on hold. With only our youngest daughter still at home, it seemed natural when two of her friends arrived to board with us, and indeed it felt as if Time was smiling benignly on us as we now laid our table for five instead of ten — and I was finally able to enroll in my Counseling Training!

However, four years later we found ourselves meeting a new challenge when an unexpected need arose for new House Parents to take over Broadstone — the school boarding Hostel. When we were approached about taking on this task, I found it very hard to consider giving up our home. Peter was reaching the end of his time with his class and had planned to make an extended visit to his family in New Zealand — while I was about to enter the final year of my counseling training. But it was clear that the situation needed a quick decision and so, despite misgivings, we decided to take on this task. Consequently the summer holidays were spent gathering those who would join us in running Broadstone, and helping to oversee the renovations that were due to take place. As the days flew by we were greatly blessed by having the very practical support of the House Father who had so recently stepped down from running Broadstone — and who happened to be a very good friend of ours!

The final packing up of our own home found us exhausted and resulted in me ending up in hospital having displaced a disc in my back. A few days later I was carried into Broadstone on a stretcher — what a way to start this new phase of our lives! In fact it turned out to be a very special time for me. Surrounded by our belongings — packed around me in black bags — I had to lie flat for a week, and the chaos of the room where I lay turned out to be a relaxing gathering place for the children to come and find me — and a wonderful opportunity for me to get to know the young people now in our care. Certainly the years that we spent as House Parents at Broadstone remain rich with memories that warmly live on in so many stories still shared to this day.

When stepping down from our role at Broadstone, we found ourselves meeting our greatest challenge. It came as a devastating shock when Peter was unexpectedly diagnosed with terminal cancer. Knowing that he had little time left on the earth, we tried together to prepare ourselves for the nature of the parting that lay ahead. We longed to feel that the deep connection that bonded us so closely would continue to support and nourish us into the future. When Peter's passing came, I did feel strengthened by this precious time we had shared together. Despite the raw grief that came to overwhelm me, I felt the path that we had longed to tread opening up before me in a way that allowed me to feel the continuing love and reassuring presence of Peter in my life.

Now eight years on, I live with my youngest daughter and her three children. The house is once more full of children — and as always with an ever-open door! When my energy starts to dwindle, and my spirits start to dip, I head to my room and gather around me the peace that I need and, since I rarely remember to put in my new hearing aids, this for the most part is possible to achieve! Finally retiring two years ago from my role as School Counselor, I do feel truly blessed with dear family and friends and a life so richly woven with precious memories.

*

Hester Renouf was yet another member of the long-meeting group in Forest Row. Eventually she moved to Sweden, and it is a special joy of working on this book to be back in contact with her.

I continued to work at the Centre for Social Development until 1985 when I moved to Sweden mainly because I wanted to work as a consultant in social situations and it was/is much easier as a woman to get work here. This I did until 2013, when it became clear that what I had to give was not as relevant anymore. I had also given many biography workshops and continued a bit longer especially for older people, where we looked at how one finds one's new tasks after retirement from ordinary work life. It was very inspiring, and I hope others continue with this.

In a workshop we organised at the turn of the century, I met two people who both brought new forces into the social work. I was part of their work for some years until one started a school to deepen the work with anthroposophy, which I joined. I have been working with this since then in many ways. I do quite a lot of administrative work in connection with the seminars we have here, and I transcribe lectures which are given in English, since this is hard for many here. I also translated lectures into Swedish, but after an accident last year, I cannot continue with this… others have taken over. We also have a study group which meets regularly with work from "Knowledge of the Higher

Worlds" and "Philosophy of Freedom" as well as many exercises in self-knowledge.

Then there are the different study groups I go to on Karma lectures and on leading thoughts of anthroposophy given by Rudolf Steiner. I am also responsible for 2 meditation groups in different parts of Sweden. So... I am involved in many anthroposophical groups and a deepening of the work here.

I go to a library group where we read novels and where I meet people who don't have any connection with anthroposophy. It is a necessary balance to the anthroposophical work.

When I travel, it is to see my children and grandchildren, 4 of them. Otherwise I travel here mostly now with the meditation work.

In writing about this, I have many memories of our work in England, which was very meaningful and helpful for me, including the hard times leading to my divorce. My ex-husband remarried but we now have a friendly contact, also with his wife.

※

There are words still to be had from one more member of the group that continues to meet when we can. I am again altering the ordering of these sharings because the question with which Margli Matthews ends her piece is one that leads into the future for all of us. Therefore, her update will come later in this chapter.

Once the Ariadne group began offering conferences and workshops, other related women's groups were started both in England and abroad. Here **Corrie Mienis** speaks about the work as it developed in Holland:

So, now something on the evolution of my life in respect to the projects we undertook in the seventies and eighties. Of course, we both remember the first Ariadne conference you organised in Forest Row. Well, being back in Holland, we enthusiastically started a women's group. And out of this group grew an Ariadne group. We gave courses, lectures, for instance, on the subjects feminine and masculine, the fourfold human being, etc. After having done that for at least ten years, our Ariadne went to sleep. A new subject came on the horizon: Huis en Gezin (**House and Family**). I stepped out.

But imagine! — our women's group that started in 1978 is still alive! Tomorrow we have our first session after the summer. Of course there were changes, but not too many. Two of us are looking out of the spiritual world to what we are doing, reading, struggling with. But nowadays we still are with eleven women. A very dear group.

※

The next offering comes from a friend with whom I shared many rich hours as our children played happily together

during the years I spent in England. Ursula Garderet has lived and worked in many countries and still travels widely, but her home is now in France.

Speaking about myself has never been easy for me; I prefer to write down my thoughts and let them grow in what I consider my secret garden. But you, Signe, and some other friends from our Forest Row period, have often challenged me with questions and a little push to take stock. So I'll simply try, trusting that the inspiration to do so will come.

There are mainly 3 large parts in my life: 22 years before being a mother, 22 years of being a full-time mother, 29 years of new professional and personal choices. That makes more than 50 years with Jacques, my "best friend." Our relationship has evolved, sometimes been shaken, but arrived at a steady being-together and sharing our days and years. There is room for the "I," for the "you" and for the "us." We are always amazed at how easily we agree in our projects and choices.

The friendship with Jacques complements my friendship with many women. I love to be a spider and build webs of women who meet, exchange and form new friendships. I never joined a women's group of any kind; for me the exchanges have to be spontaneous and free. Every woman I meet adds a new dimension and colour to the fabric around me.

Our children and grandchildren are my joy, and I thank them for being what they are. They grew and helped me to grow at the same time.

My work in and with nature gives me a lot of satisfaction. It is "creation" in the true sense. I need to create beauty around me — in the garden, the kitchen, in my crafts and projects.

Times of bereavement and illness have made me stronger. I try to take time to listen to people who are not as fortunate as I am, to have always an open ear close by.

Patience, courage and inner strength, are the things I still wish to develop in the autumn of my life.

*

The writer of the following piece asked that it be kept anonymous. What she shares is honest, painful and very important, with various aspects that I imagine will be familiar to many. It addresses some of the challenges of aging and focuses on a particularly difficult moment in time; but as this friend wrote in a separate note, *"Things might change — which is what I am going to strive for!"*

Having reacted enthusiastically to the idea of writing something about my life at 80, I find I am in a dilemma. It's as if I live two different lives, side by side. The one that the outside world sees, but if I am brutally honest, igne Eklund Schaefer

the other is not straight forward, and I'm not sure if I am brave enough to voice it.

How strange that this should come at a time when I am struggling in so many ways to make sense of my life, struggling in my marriage, struggling with 'old age' and all the physical ailments that brings, struggling to come to terms with the thought of death and dying, in spite of my Anthroposophical knowledge (small as it is). This has caught me at a deep 'low' and I am feeling very lost and don't know where to turn.

Because of circumstances and my inability to solve them, I am reacting emotionally as a child might, losing my temper, becoming frustrated, fearful and worst of all, angry. I don't know why I feel such anger, (something I must get to the bottom of!) After these outbursts, I feel deep guilt, depression and hopelessness, that there will never be joy again. I can't even take joy in my lovely family, as they have been absent from my life for so long, no grandchildren near by to lift one's spirit.

My 'outer' life is very fulfilling, helping friends less fortunate than myself who have Alzheimer's or are almost blind; a lovely knitting group, which I have wanted for years; a Gentle Ballet class for the elderly, which is wonderful, and many village activities, which are very rewarding; wonderful friends of 50 years standing; a home built by my husband 50 years ago; just enough money to keep our heads above water, though not much for luxuries. In 56 years I have only had one holiday where I didn't have to cook!

Ah, but here's the rub, how easily, for example, in my relationship with my husband, things can deteriorate into meaningless irritations. Retirement has changed the dynamic of living in one space together, and we often don't see eye to eye about many practical things. These petty things, which I KNOW are not important become intolerable at times. I have been trying so hard to ignore, find humour, just quietly re-wash the dirty glasses, etc., but I can't let it go and then am accused of pettiness and obsessiveness. How to adapt when we have different standards?

I still love him, we share so many important elements and history together, but this is driving me mad! And in many ways old age is so cruel... when you chance on photos of what you were like as a young handsome couple and now, false teeth, hearing aids that don't work properly, saggy tummies, loss of hair or grey hair, and the most challenging thing at the moment, finding a purpose in life, when the outer world doesn't need you anymore. I am fortunate in that I have a passion in my craft life but suddenly my husband is not needed anymore in his field of work, which has been his whole life. I don't think his love of gardening is going to fill that huge hole.

It saddens me greatly to be feeling this way, and I just pray that we can re-find JOY in our lives... but it takes two to tango!

✳

Stephanie Westphal and I first met in England over four decades ago, then lived far apart for many years, but now we are both living in New England. It is a joy to occasionally meet for a meal or a visit, also with our husbands, and sometimes even with our grown children.

Now the baby I wrote of long ago is thirty-two years old, and she is traveling all over the US on a concert tour with her boyfriend, who is a musician. She is a strong, brave and vulnerable human being, as are all of my children. She cares deeply about other people and has worked steadily since her freshman year of college, as a filmmaker, a PA, managing the New York office of Students for a Free Tibet, and most recently as a beekeeper in Austin.

As for me at seventy, I cannot describe myself as happy, but rather I feel complete and full of a surprising contentment. I have come to my center and cherish my inner life. I knew that I needed to retire (from nursing) when I realized that I had no time to sit and stare anymore, and that my work was my life. Eight months into retirement, I would describe myself as a contemplative. I am so grateful for the closeness of our family, and for my husband's friendship and support.

Since I retired I have been simplifying everything, and I am trying to recreate a monastic way of life in my every day. We live close to our one precious grandchild and I am amazed at how different being a grandmother is from being a mother. This child is my friend and I feel as though I have known her much longer than her five years of life.

What a joy and a blessing it was to be a young mother in England, to push the pram through the village to buy my groceries, to walk my children to school down the "cow path," and to have many good friends to chat to and share meals with. I still keep in touch with several of the wonderful women who were my friends then, and I am touched to be asked to write a bit about my life by one of them.

*

Some of my American friends settled down in England, but Lee Sturgeon Day went the other way; originally from England she eventually made her home in California. As you will read, her world travelling has not ceased over the years. She is another friend who has been a leading voice in the development of biography work, in the US and further afield.

I am probably double the age I was when I wrote Signe, at a particularly dark time in my life.

Now, in my late 70's, this is one of the best decades. One lovely feature is that my son, who works for the UN is taking me back to countries I travelled through in my 20's. A mirroring, half a century later: Far East, Middle East, even a new continent, Africa.

At a workshop I gave in Beirut a few years ago, I brought an exercise to recall our adolescence and note three things we had hoped to achieve or experience in the life ahead. I wrote: 1) Travel, 2) Write a book, 3) Meet a true love.

I have written books and lived and travelled in many countries. A participant then asked if I had met a true love, and I burst into tears. "Yes, it is my granddaughter, Kaia." I got exactly what I hoped for, plus a few things I hadn't bargained for: cancer, a year or so of total silence due to a botched vocal cord surgery, lots of friendships, lots of laughter, quite some sorrows. Even a second true love when my next granddaughter arrived.

Now, moving towards the end of the tracks, I have entered my "Mary Oliver" phase, walking slowly among the trees, at least those that still survive the California fires, trying to look and listen better, trying to bring something positive to the small corner of the planet, the cosmos, that I inhabit. And in the past year I have had enormous pleasure telling people I might not meet again this time round what each brought into my life. I met with two from those dark days I first mentioned. Neither had the slightest idea how each was an utter "lifesaver' for me. I met a third, in Japan last year. We had one hour together, our exchange was deep and remarkable, knowing too it will be our last. These are opportunities I don't want to miss. And last, but absolutely not least, I want to spend as much time as I can with the younger generations who bear the challenging future of humanity in their hands and hearts.

My granddaughter Satya wrote out her life goals when she was four. They were: 1. Save the Trees. 2. Save the Llamas. 3. Save the Penguins. 4. Stop people killing each other. 5. THAT'S IT!

Mine are a little more modest, but then I have a lot less time. So THAT'S IT, for me.

*

Now we come to the words by Margli Matthews. As I mentioned before, she was a member of the women's group that met weekly in Forest Row for many years and still gets together when we can. Margli has been a leader in the development of Biography work internationally, including as visiting faculty for many years in the Biography and Social Art training that I founded in the late 1990's in New York.

Signe, I am so grateful that you opened that box, and found those letters ... the words that moved between you and so many, recording a special time in our lives, expressing our questions and experiences about being women, wives, mothers, friends, about our dreams, joys, dilemmas and struggles.

Looking back, it feels like my whole adult life began then. I woke up. In 1968 I had found my way from Berkeley, California, where I had been studying literature (and the radical student politics of the time) to Emerson College. There I met anthroposophy, met and married my husband and began to make my home in England. By 1973 I had two young children, was living in Forest Row and my husband had begun teaching at Emerson College.

Signe Eklund Schaefer

The time in my life from 28 and 42 (1973 — 1987), meeting and sharing with women friends, face to face and then with you through letters (and occasional phone calls) was fundamental to my becoming. All the words given and received, building imaginations of who we were and could become, supported and encouraged me in my development — in my family life and in my search to find myself and task.

Our women's group that met weekly for 7 years completely informed these years of my life. We studied together and shared the events and questions of our lives. Gradually we supported others to form groups; we gave talks and ran workshops and courses on biography, family life, parenting, relationships, masculine and feminine, social renewal and the reawakening of the feminine. Writing this, I wonder, who were these young women?! In time we named this work Ariadne. Some of the fruits of this work were gathered in the books *Lifeways: Working with Family Questions*, and *Ariadne's Awakening, Taking up the Threads of Consciousness*, and a journal by that name that we put out between 1978 and 1983.

For me, meeting and working together over these years was a path of inner and outer development, a practice ground and training — in adult education, biography work and psychotherapy. Most of all, perhaps, it was about relationship, about what a meeting could be: the transforming power of interest and attention of one to another, the potential of seeing and being seen. This was a blessing in my life, a sustaining and inspiring source for my personal and professional life. Receiving it, I wanted to give it out. It led me to my professional path.

In these years I began teaching and carrying the Foundation Year at Emerson College and facilitating courses on biography and 'the helping conversation' at the Centre for Social Development. Then in 1988, I took part in the first counselling training offered at the Centre. The questions and crises that my students were bringing to me, together with my own struggles and dilemmas, had been preparing me. I wanted to be able to offer people more ongoing help to meet the range and depth of their questions. Together with many others, I had been waiting for this course — for the development of an approach to counseling out of anthroposophy.

In 1992, soon after finishing the training, I was asked, together with Anita Charton, to direct and carry the further development of this training, which we called Biographical Counselling. In time we established the Biography and Social Development Trust to hold and develop the Training in Biographical Counselling and other initiatives connected with biography work and human encounter out of the anthroposophy.

In the following 21 years, I was engaged in developing and running the Training in the UK. In these years, I also mentored the development of the Training in Russia and contributed to the work of biography and biographical counselling in other courses and trainings in various countries. I also had a private biographical counselling and supervision practice.

Carrying and developing the Training in Biographical Counselling and practicing as a biographical counsellor and supervisor has been a calling… and a gift and privilege — to hear so many peoples' stories, to witness people growing, taking hold of their lives and becoming creative.

At present I continue my counselling/supervision practice, teach sometimes, live with the current questions of our world, and enjoy time with my husband, children and grandchildren, and the wider circles of family and friends. With their encouragement, I am trying to create more time to pause and listen… and wonder what this phase of life is opening and asking of me. I feel graced by the opportunity to be able to continue to meet with a number of dear women friends who first met so long ago, and to gather to our many years of sharing the theme of growing older and the question of karma, the interweaving of our destinies and the power of the words that we wove between us. I am living with the question: who are we to each other — past, present and future?

*

I have woven aspects of my own life update throughout this book, but following on my friends I will touch a few more strands in my own ongoing story. Like some of the others, my main work was in adult education — first at Emerson College, then once our family returned to the

States, at Sunbridge College where I directed Foundation Studies for many years. The gender theme that came so alive in my years in England continued to inform my life and ways of working, as well as my study and teaching of human development. It was such a privilege to work with adult students, watching them find their next steps, learning with them ever more about the mysteries, responsibilities, and necessities in our life on earth, and also about the possibilities of freedom at this time in human evolution. In 1997, in addition to my other work at Sunbridge, I founded a professional development training for people wanting to work in the emerging field of Biography and Social Art. Both the training and other public aspects of the work now continue to grow through the Center for Biography and Social Art.[1]

During the over fifty years of our marriage, my husband and I have also often been colleagues, at Emerson and Sunbridge and also giving workshops together in many parts of the world. Being able to work on social or biographical questions with people in Brazil, China,

---

1   The Center for Biography and Social Art celebrates the threefold human being — body, soul and spirit; encourages reverence for the uniqueness of every life journey; illuminates the mysteries of human life in earthly gesture and spiritual depth; and practices authentic human encounter. The Center fulfills its mission through adult education programs and events, research, professional training and networking, and community and client support. <http://biographysocialart.org/>

Norway, Hungary and many places in between has been a great gift in our lives. Along the way our children grew up and now have families of their own. They and their partners, and our grandchildren and great-grandchildren bring us renewing joy and hope for the future. After all my years of fascination with questions of human development, it is a particular pleasure at this stage of my life, to experience how each member of the family moves through universal life phases in their own very individual and awe-inspiring ways. Not surprisingly, I am particularly interested now in the process of aging.

＊

Margli Matthews asked two important questions in the words she shared, and I would like to look at both of them as this book comes to a close. In thinking back on our women's group in the 1970's, Margli asked the question, "Who were these young women?!" Perhaps this is a version of what we all ask ourselves when we look back and wonder how, and maybe also why, we did so many different things in the early and middle years of our adult lives. Who was I? Who was there with me? And who have I become? What threads moved through each of our lives, pulling us this way and that, guiding us toward life-changing encounters, drawing us to half-open doorways that invited or sometimes pushed us to move forward? Can we remember gazing through windows that offered a glimpse of still far off possibilities? As we grow older, such questions naturally arise, and they can help illuminate the arc of our unique life story. They also show ever more clearly that who we have become is completely interwoven with the others in our lives, is actually dependent on what others brought out of us — the challenges, obstacles and gifts they offered through their attention, neglect, needs, encouragement, restriction, or support.

Margli ended her piece with another question, one which addresses our lives in relationship, in time, and even over several lifetimes: "who are we to each other — past, present and future?" She was referring to those of us who have continued to meet, when we can, for more than forty-five years. This has become for us a karmic question; it arose when we were younger, but now feels necessary and important to consider even without the expectation of clear or finished answers. There are clues to be followed and common themes to be explored. We have never doubted that we matter to each other or that we know and feel known by the others. Since we all feel the truth of reincarnation, we do not shy away from inklings of past connections, and we look forward to meeting each other in the future in ways we cannot yet imagine but do not doubt.

I would like to extend this karmic question beyond our small group, and even beyond the intimacy of familiar relationships. Contemporary life challenges us on so many fronts, not only in our personal lives but also as global citizens. Every day we meet questions of justice, truth, and inter-dependence with our fellow human beings and with the social structures and physical environment that surround us. The future of what it means to be human rests with all of us. "Who are we to each other — past, present and future?"

What if reincarnation is indeed a reality of human life? Would a sense for destiny change the way we interact with others or how we exercise responsibility in relating to the Earth? Would we be encouraged to create social and economic conditions that would better serve the health and well being of all? Even without the idea of karmic consequences resulting from our thoughts and deeds, do not the complex and often-painful realities of life today call us ever and again to meet each other, the Earth, and ourselves with an earnest and loving seriousness? Sometimes the call is loud and insistent; often it is drowned out by the bombarding confusion of modern life. How can we help each other attend to this call?

In my own life, friendships have been central to my becoming and in helping me stay awake to the needs around me. Given my particular biography, as this book makes clear, letters played a large part in this. They took time to write, and so I experienced the work of caring. Receiving them brought an awareness of being supported and a joy that was not to be taken for granted. The act of writing itself helped bring into words my questions, feelings, and a growing sense of individual responsibility. Letters — in the sending and receiving, in the writing and the reading — brought into focus the activity of self-reflection and even more, the importance of the other, of relationship, and the value of authentic soul communication.

As we come to the end of this book, I would like to encourage you to write a letter to someone you love. You could see it as an act of connection, an opportunity to hold the other in your inner being and write whatever it is you want to say to them, to consciously and heartfully give your words to this one other. Your friend will receive what you share from yourself, including perhaps questions that are stirring within you. As you reach toward your friend with trust in the relationship, you may find yourself within a time-extended conversation.

I do not imagine that in our age of instant communication, letter writing will again become what it was in the past. That time is now gone. But precisely in our age of so many virtual exchanges, it becomes ever more important to find ways to practice building, nurturing, and honoring real and loving relationships. To write a letter is to step through the isolation that is such a part of our times and to ease for a moment the loneliness of another. It is one way to enliven a particular relationship and in so doing to serve human connection more generally. The activity itself has rippling effect.

In writing and receiving letters, we practice bridging distances and differences. Whether on paper or face-to-face, a genuine exchange is what matters. Offering each other our heart-filled words, and receiving what comes from the other with living interest — these are small but also mighty acts. Our listening becomes a nourishing and uniting force, and the gift of our words a deed of love.

Acknowledgments

This book would not exist without my friends and the life-rich letters they wrote to me so long ago. My gratitude for our friendship is ongoing. I am especially happy that the book has made possible reconnections and deepening contact between several of us. Many warm thanks to Dede Bark, Stephanie Cooper, Ursula Garderet, Karen Gierlach, Sherry Jennings, Christa Kaufmann, Nancy Lippincott, Noela Maletz, Margli Matthews, Corrie Mienis, Marcia Putnam, Hester Renouf, Ellen Robin, Libby Sheen, Lee Sturgeon-Day, and Stephanie Westphal. Linda Norris and Tessa Chao are no longer alive, but my gratitude and love for them both is as strong as ever. I am sorry that I was unable to connect with Welmoed or Lisa, but I am glad their words are in this book.

I also want to thank friends who were not part of this letter writing — most of whom I met since the time when the letters were written — who read part or all of the book in draft form and made very helpful comments. Their encouragement for the project meant a great deal to me. Much gratitude to Kathleen Bowen, Jennifer Brooks Quinn, Kathleen Hughes, Jan Hutchinson, Jenny Koenig, Patricia Rubano, Mary Schaefer, Patti Smith, and Robin Zeamer.

Jennifer Browdy and Jana Laiz at Green Fire Press welcomed this project from the beginning, and I thank them and their colleagues for all the work they did to bring the book to print.

My daughter Karin and my son Stefan have unmarked cameo appearances in several of the excerpts in this book. In those long-ago days they were my daily companions, and the gift of being their mother has continued to deepen over the years. Thank you to them both and to their own beloved families for all the learning and all the joy. My husband Chris also figured in the letters, and, of course, much more in the searching and the growing that was going on for me all those years ago, and ever since. I am renewingly grateful for his enthusiastic interest and support for this project, and for so much else throughout the years.

Signe Eklund Schaefer is the author of *Why on Earth? —
Biography and the Practice of Human Becoming*. She was the
founding director of a professional development program
in Biography and Social Art, one of several activities of the
Center for Biography and Social Art. A teacher of adults for
many decades, she has been a student of life for as long as
she can remember. Her desire to know more about the multiple dimensions of human development led her as a young
person to the work of Rudolf Steiner and to Waldorf education. She directed Foundation Studies at Sunbridge College
in New York for over twenty years, and was on the faculty
of Emerson College in England before that. She co-au-
thored *Ariadne's Awakening*, a book on gender questions
and co-edited the parenting book *More Lifeways*. A mother,
grandmother, and great-grandmother, she now lives in Great
Barrington, MA with her husband Christopher Schaefer.

About Green Fire Press

Green Fire Press is an independent publishing company dedicated to supporting authors in producing and distributing high-quality books in fiction or non-fiction, poetry or prose.

Find out more at **Greenfirepress.com**.

Other Green Fire Press titles you may also enjoy:

A Short Course In Happiness After Loss, by Maria Sirois, PsyD.

A lyrical gem of a book, combining positive psychology with the wisdom necessary to thrive when facing life's harshest moments, rising through pain into a steady, resilient and open heart.

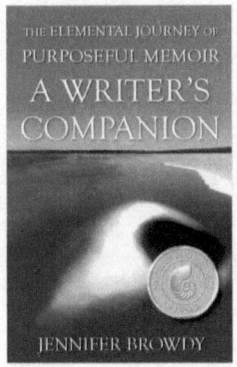

The Elemental Journey of Purposeful Memoir: A Writer's Companion, by Jennifer Browdy, PhD.

Month-by-month guidance for memoir writers.

Winner of the 2017 Nautilus Silver Award.

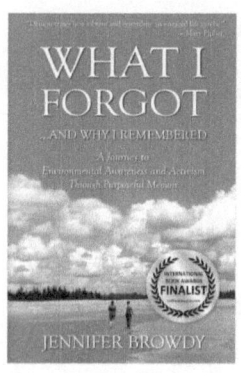

What I Forgot…and Why I Remembered: A Journey to Environmental Awareness and Activism Through Purposeful Memoir, by Jennifer Browdy, PhD.

"Inspires us to see how we can reclaim our lives for the sake of life on Earth" –Joanna Macy.

Finalist for the 2018 International Book Award.

Writing Fire: Celebrating the Power of Women's Words, edited by Jennifer Browdy, Jana Laiz and Sahra Bateson Brubeck.

More than 75 passionate women writers share their voices and visions in this powerful anthology.

Nature, Culture, and the Sacred: A Woman Listens For Leadership, by Nina Simons

Bioneers co-founder Nina Simons offers inspiration for anyone who aspires to grow into their own unique form of leadership with resilience and joy. Winner of the 2018 Nautilus Gold Award.

Wisdom Lessons: Spirited Guidance from an Ojibwe Great-Grandmother, by Mary Lyons

The culmination of a lifetime steeped in Indigenous spiritual traditions, Grandmother Mary offers invaluable lessons for anyone interested in living in alignment with their higher self.